W9-DBS-144

DISCARD

Prosecuting the President

PROSECUTING THE PRESIDENT

How Special Prosecutors Hold Presidents
Accountable and Protect the Rule of Law

ANDREW COAN

OXFORD
UNIVERSITY PRESS

OXFORD
UNIVERSITY PRESS

Oxford University Press is a department of the University of Oxford. It furthers
the University's objective of excellence in research, scholarship, and education
by publishing worldwide. Oxford is a registered trade mark of Oxford University
Press in the UK and certain other countries.

Published in the United States of America by Oxford University Press
198 Madison Avenue, New York, NY 10016, United States of America.

Library of Congress Cataloging-in-Publication Data
Names: Coan, Andrew, author.
Title: Prosecuting the president : how special prosecutors hold presidents accountable and
protect the rule of law / Andrew Coan, Oxford University Press.
Description: New York, NY : Oxford University Press, [2019] | Includes index.
Identifiers: LCCN 2018039056 (print) | LCCN 2018039684 (ebook) |
ISBN 9780190943875 (Universal PDF) | ISBN 9780190943882 (E-pub) |
ISBN 9780190943868 (hardback : alk. paper)
Subjects: LCSH: Special prosecutors—United States. | Presidents—United States. |
Misconduct in office—United States. | Executive power—United States. |
Obstruction of justice—United States. | Governmental investigations—United States. |
Rule of law—United States. | United States—Politics and government.
Classification: LCC KF5107.5 (ebook) | LCC KF5107.5 .C63 2019 (print) | DDC 345.73/01—dc23
LC record available at https://lccn.loc.gov/2018039056

9 8 7 6 5 4 3 2 1

Printed by Sheridan Books, Inc., United States of America

To my children, who give me hope

I am the only one that matters.

—**President Donald J. Trump**

Whether we shall continue to be a Government of laws and not of men is now for Congress and ultimately the American people.

—**Watergate Special Prosecutor Archibald Cox**

CONTENTS

Introduction

"I shall resign the presidency effective at noon tomorrow." With these words, spoken just after 9 p.m. on August 8, 1974, Richard Nixon ended an American tragedy. In its place, he created a mystery. The most powerful man in the most powerful country on earth had been driven from office by a special prosecutor he could have fired at any time. How could this happen? Behind this mystery lay another, even deeper one. Why was such a subordinate official entrusted with investigating the president of the United States?

Two hundred years earlier, Americans fought a revolution to overthrow the maxim that "the King can do no wrong." In its place, they enshrined the fundamental principle that no one, not even the president, is above the law. Few ideas have been more central to the nation's democratic self-image. The words "Equal Justice Under Law" are engraved above the entrance to the United States Supreme Court.

Yet no law required Richard Nixon to appoint an outside prosecutor when credible evidence emerged that he had committed a crime. When Nixon chose to appoint such a prosecutor voluntarily, no law barred him from shutting down the investigation to save his own skin. How could the nation have left its sacred ideals so weakly protected?

Since Nixon's resignation, these mysteries have only deepened. In 1978, Congress created a strong independent prosecutor who could not easily be fired by the president. But this solution quickly proved controversial, and Congress scrapped it after the impeachment of President Bill Clinton in 1999. Today, the United States is right back where it was when Nixon resigned. Special prosecutors still strike fear into the hearts of presidents, who can still fire them at any time.

This book unravels the mystery. More specifically, it answers three questions. First, how did special prosecutors come to exercise significant power, despite serving purely at the pleasure of the president? Second, why has the United States rejected stronger institutional safeguards of the sort embraced by other advanced democracies? Third, what does this history means for special prosecutors today?

The short answer to all three is that special prosecutors function as catalysts for democracy. By raising the visibility of presidential misconduct, they enable the American people to hold the president accountable for his actions. But special prosecutors, just like presidents, can abuse their power. To guard against this risk, the president retains the power to fire a special prosecutor at any time. If he exercises that power corruptly or capriciously, special prosecutors have no legal remedy. But they are not unprotected. The president must ultimately answer to the American people. This has proved a surprisingly powerful deterrent.

The first special prosecutor was appointed by President Ulysses S. Grant in 1875 to investigate a bribery scandal involving his close friends and associates. Ever since, presidents of both parties have appointed special prosecutors and empowered them to operate with unusual independence. In short order, such appointments became a standard method for neutralizing political scandals and demonstrating the president's commitment to the rule of law.

This long, mostly forgotten history shows that special prosecutors can do much to protect the rule of law under the right circumstances. It also shows that they are fallible. Many have been thwarted by the substantial challenges of investigating a sitting president and his close associates. Some have abused the powers entrusted to them. Yet such cases are rare. More often, the specter of a runaway special prosecutor has functioned as a tool of presidential propaganda.

Most important, this history shows that special prosecutors are only as powerful as the American people want them to be. They are quite incapable of saving us from ourselves. Any hope to the contrary is wishful thinking.

The first half of this book traces the history of special prosecutors from 1875 to 2018. The stories recounted in these chapters encompass a stolen presidential nomination, shady international arms deals, huge piles of cash in suitcases, and more. The quintessentially American cast of characters includes Ulysses S. Grant, the Civil War hero and president; Edward Doheny, the powerful oil baron who inspired the movie *There Will Be Blood*; and a corrupt secretary of the interior named Albert Fall, who carried a revolver and would have fit in nicely at the O.K. Corral.

Broadly speaking, the arc of this history bends toward the rule of law, but its progress has been far from smooth. In their Gilded Age infancy, special prosecutors were often stymied by broad public cynicism and endemic government corruption. Gradually, the worst forms of corruption grew less pervasive, and public norms for official conduct became more robust. By the 1970s, those norms were strong enough that a special prosecutor investigation exposing their flagrant violation could drive a twice-elected president from office.

For two generations, Richard Nixon's downfall served as a warning for any president tempted to fire a special prosecutor or otherwise flout the rule of law. By global and historical standards, American democratic norms remain strong today. But the rise of populism and political polarization is a worrisome trend—for future special prosecutor investigations and for American democracy more generally.

The second half of this book turns from history to law. Chapters 6–9 explore several of the great constitutional questions that arise in special prosecutor investigations. These include whether the president can be charged with a crime (probably not); whether the president can be compelled to testify before a grand jury (possibly); whether the president can obstruct justice (almost certainly yes); and whether the president can fire a special prosecutor (yes, at least for now). In one form or another, all four of these questions have arisen in every special prosecutor investigation of a sitting president.

In each case, law is only one of part of the story. The stakes are so high, the legal precedents so few, and the power of courts so limited that politics matters greatly, too. This puts the lawyers on both sides in a peculiar position. They can and do make traditional legal arguments, citing the text of the Constitution and Supreme Court opinions. But in most cases, it is anybody's guess what a court might do—or whether it will do anything at all. Many legal questions are therefore resolved through ad hoc negotiation. In such negotiations, leverage is all-important. The best leverage comes from having the court of public opinion on your side.

This may be the most important and least understood aspect of special prosecutor investigations. To misquote Justice Oliver Wendell Holmes, the law is not a "brooding omnipresence in the sky" that supplies clear answers to all disputes. Rather, in the highly charged context of investigating the president, the law is a complex form of prognostication. It combines "what the courts will do in fact"—Holmes again—and what the public will allow the parties to get away with. This gives ordinary Americans enormous power and enormous responsibility.[1]

The stories recounted in these chapters encompass dramatic Supreme Court showdowns, Oval Office trysts, Mexican money laundering, and more. The cast of characters includes Alexia Morrison, a young mother making her first argument before the United States Supreme Court; Paul Manafort, the international man of mystery who chaired Donald Trump's presidential campaign; and the team of Ivy League whiz kids that brought down Richard Nixon. Broadly speaking, these stories attest to the power of special prosecutors to hold presidents accountable. They also underscore the formidable obstacles that special prosecutors face. Most of all, they demonstrate the central role of democratic politics in determining the success or failure of special prosecutor investigations.

The history and law of special prosecutors—and, thus, the two halves of this book—teach a common lesson. At their best, special prosecutors function as avatars of the people channeling an unfocused popular will to safeguard the rule of law. But special prosecutors can function effectively only if the people care about holding the president accountable. If a president thinks he can fire a special prosecutor without incurring serious political damage, he has the power to do it. Presidents Ulysses Grant, Harry Truman, and Richard Nixon all exercised this power. Grant and Truman escaped without serious consequence. Nixon did not.

Ultimately, only the American people can decide whether the president is above the law. At any given moment, this question can seem like a purely partisan one. Anyone who likes the current president—whoever he is—will be tempted to view legal constraints on presidential power as an irritating inconvenience. All Americans, however, have a profound stake in preserving the "government of laws and not of men" passed down to us by previous generations.

The alternative is a system in which the president is "the only one that matters." That sort of despotism is just what the American founders fought a revolution to overthrow. It is also what many of our ancestors fled their home countries to escape. Special prosecutors can help to ward off this threat, but only with our help. This book provides the information every American needs to perform this civic duty intelligently and responsibly.

1

A Special Kind of Prosecutor

When California lawyer Donald Smaltz agreed to serve as a special prosecutor, he had no idea what he was getting himself into. The date was September 9, 1994. His charge was to investigate bribery allegations against President Bill Clinton's secretary of agriculture, Mike Espy. Smaltz assumed the job would last about six months. Five years later, he was still on the case. An experienced federal prosecutor, Smaltz had also practiced law in the private sector for almost two decades. He was nobody's idea of a legal novice. But nothing in his long career had prepared him for the colossal challenges of serving as a special prosecutor.

Those challenges stem directly from the unique role that special prosecutors play in the American constitutional system. Their job is to ensure that no person, not even the highest government official, is above the law. They do this by investigating and prosecuting alleged wrongdoing by the president and his close associates. This work is vital to a healthy democracy. It also poses exceptional challenges. Those challenges—and the high stakes of surmounting them—are what make special prosecutors special.

The Basics

To prevent political interference with their work, special prosecutors are generally appointed from outside the government.
Sometimes, the president selects them directly. Other times, he
delegates their selection to the attorney general, the presidential
lieutenant who heads the Justice Department and supervises all
ordinary federal prosecutors. Once appointed, special prosecutors
enjoy unusual independence from the normal Justice Department
hierarchy. The precise scope of this independence has varied over
time. But all special prosecutors have operated free from direct,
day-to-day oversight by the attorney general or the president.

Nevertheless, the attorney general retains the power to fire a
special prosecutor, a decision that is not reviewable in any court. If
the president wishes to fire a special prosecutor and the attorney
general refuses, the president has two choices. He can back off,
or he can fire the attorney general and install someone who will
carry out his wishes. This puts special prosecutors in the peculiar
and unenviable position of investigating their ultimate boss and his
close associates.

To carry out this difficult charge, special prosecutors are granted
the same formal powers as ordinary federal prosecutors, with one
crucially important difference. For special prosecutors, the power
to investigate and authorize criminal charges is confined to particular persons or suspected crimes. In technical legal parlance,
special prosecutors have limited, rather than general, jurisdiction.
Today, that jurisdiction is defined by the attorney general, who
provides special prosecutors with "a specific factual statement of
the matter to be investigated." By contrast, ordinary federal prosecutors, known as U.S. attorneys, possess unqualified or "plenary"
authority to investigate and prosecute any federal crime within
their geographical districts.[1]

This difference has profound practical implications for the conduct of special prosecutor investigations. It forces special prosecutors to build a functioning team from scratch. It tips off potential targets of the investigation in advance. It sets the stage for legal battles over the special prosecutor's authority. It also encourages special prosecutors to investigate their targets with relentless, sometimes obsessive, focus. Most important, it places special prosecutors squarely in the public spotlight. That gives the president's allies a strong incentive to discredit special prosecutors. It also enables the public to hold the president accountable. Only if the American people take this responsibility seriously can special prosecutors do their job effectively.

Assembling a Team

The first challenge Donald Smaltz confronted after taking up the baton as special prosecutor was a basic one. He would have to create and staff a functioning prosecutor's office from scratch. A new special prosecutor, Smaltz later recalled, "has no copy machine, no office, no staff, no lawyers, no agents, no books, no computers—not even a telephone." Eventually, Smaltz procured a temporary space in the basement of the Thurgood Marshall Federal Judiciary Building, one mile north of the Capitol. From this "closet"—Smaltz's word for it—he began the formidable task of recruiting top lawyers and investigators to join his prosecutorial team.[2]

This is an experience every special prosecutor goes through at the outset of the job. As a Californian, Smaltz probably found it more daunting than most. But even for old Washington hands, the burden of setting up an office from scratch is a heavy one. Special prosecutors are free to recruit current federal prosecutors and generally do so. But they still lack the established relationships and institutional memory that ordinary prosecutors enjoy. To maintain their independence, special prosecutors are compelled to jump through extra hoops before drawing on the resources of the Justice Department and other federal agencies. In some cases, the Justice Department and other law enforcement agencies are themselves under investigation.

Meanwhile, special prosecutors face great pressure to get their investigations up and running quickly. The Silicon Valley business cliché is apt. Special prosecutors are expected to build a plane while flying it.

The difficulties inherent in such an undertaking are compounded by the uncertain duration of special prosecutor investigations. Recruits know the work is temporary, but they do not know how long it will last. For bright and ambitious young lawyers, this means stepping off the ladder of professional advancement. For more experienced lawyers, it often means stepping away from a lucrative law firm partnership. It may also require relocating their families and personal lives to Washington, all for an unknown period of time.

Reflecting on his own experiences in office, Smaltz summed up the challenge nicely: "a potential new hire's first question usually is: 'How long will I be working on this investigation?' Response: 'I don't know.' The second question is: 'Where will it be housed?' Response: 'I don't know.' The third question is: 'When will you know?' Response: 'I'm not sure.'" In the face of such uncertainty, many otherwise well-qualified lawyers are reluctant to take the job. It can therefore take as long as a year before a special prosecutor's team is fully staffed and functioning smoothly. Even then, the staff is likely to turn over at an unusual rate, as personal and financial considerations drive crucial team members to leave. The inefficiencies and delay that come with bringing new staff up to speed midstream are substantial.

This puts special prosecutors in a formidably difficult position right from the outset, but it also carries certain advantages. Rather than being asked to fly a plane that someone else picked out, special prosecutors have the flexibility to design their own. They can recruit and hire lawyers of their own choosing, with expertise and experience specially suited to the investigation at hand. The opportunity to investigate high-profile wrongdoing by senior government officials is generally exciting enough to attract the interest of many talented lawyers. This is especially true for younger lawyers, who tend to be more adventurous and to have greater personal and financial flexibility.

Early in his investigation of Watergate, special prosecutor Archibald Cox asked Nashville lawyer James F. Neal to join his team. A former U.S. attorney who cut his teeth prosecuting Jimmy Hoffa, Neal was not an easy sell. He had recently formed his own law firm at age forty-three, after a career devoted to public service. To accept a position in Washington would require a large financial sacrifice and a major interruption of his personal affairs. But like many lawyers, Neal had an acute sense of history. The chance to be a part of it was a powerful draw. He was also a little star-struck by Cox, who had served as solicitor general of the United States when Neal was just a junior prosecutor. "I guess the excitement of the Watergate case, the interest of it, was my pinch of greed," Neal reflected. "When it came down to it, I just didn't feel I could turn Archie down if he felt he needed me."[3]

Many other lawyers tapped for service in special prosecutor investigations have felt a similar mix of excitement and public duty. Largely for this reason, special prosecutors have generally assembled extremely impressive legal teams. Many members of those teams have gone on to illustrious careers in their own right. Recent examples include Deputy Attorney General Rod Rosenstein, Secretary of Health and Human Services Alex Azar, and Supreme

Court justice Brett Kavanaugh. All worked under special prosecutor Kenneth Starr during his investigation of President Bill Clinton in the mid-1990s.

The Element of Surprise

Anyone who has seen the HBO series *The Wire* knows that surprise and secrecy are hugely important factors in a criminal investigation. The Justice Department manual for prosecutors devotes an entire chapter to the importance of investigative secrecy. When investigators and prosecutors can gather evidence and interview potential witnesses in secret, suspects have less chance to cover their tracks. When an investigation becomes public in its early stages, the ability of suspects to coordinate and obstruct the investigation dramatically increases. This is especially true for complex public corruption cases of the sort that most special prosecutors are called on to investigate. As the Justice Department manual sums it up, "the covert or undercover investigation" is the single most important investigative technique for attacking public corruption.[4]

Ordinary investigators and prosecutors, working outside the media spotlight, are frequently able to maintain investigative secrecy until quite late in the game. For special prosecutors, it is rarely possible to do so. Often, public outrage over a political scandal is what leads to the appointment of a special prosecutor in the first place. This greatly complicates a special prosecutor's job, as does the fact that special prosecutors nearly always inherit ongoing investigations. Not infrequently, the investigations they inherit were commenced by the very officials or departments the special prosecutors are charged with investigating. They might as well begin every investigation by shouting, "Ready or not, here I come!"[5]

When Archibald Cox took over as Watergate special prosecutor in May 1973, he inherited an especially sensitive ongoing investigation. Led by U.S. attorney Earl Silbert, a team of federal prosecutors in Washington had discovered a criminal conspiracy implicating Richard Nixon's top White House advisors. The object of the conspiracy was to cover up the Nixon campaign's involvement in the burglary of Democratic National Committee headquarters at the Watergate office complex on June 17, 1972.

Silbert and his team had moved aggressively to investigate the officials involved. In fact, it was their investigation that triggered Cox's appointment as special prosecutor. But at the outset, Cox and his team could not afford to trust anyone. Perhaps Silbert's Justice Department superiors had pressured him to slow-walk the investigation. This possibility could not be ruled out. Some of those officials were suspects in the very conspiracy their department was supposedly investigating.[6]

Eventually, Cox concluded that Silbert and his team had behaved with integrity. The same could not be said for Silbert's immediate superior. Assistant Attorney General Henry Petersen, it emerged, had secretly relayed inside information to President Nixon for several weeks. It is difficult to imagine a more damaging breach of secrecy. The president would eventually become the investigation's prime target. Thanks to Petersen, the president and his lawyers knew every move the prosecution was planning and every piece of evidence it had collected. The closest parallel in an ordinary federal prosecution would be for a member of the prosecutorial team secretly to accept bribes from the defendant in exchange for inside information.[7]

Such flagrant misconduct is exceedingly rare, but in a special prosecutor investigation the lines demarcating ethical conduct are far less clear. The president and top Justice Department officials are both the chief law enforcement officers of the United States and potential suspects. By design, special prosecutors operate independently of these officials, but they also depend on the Justice

Department for resources, information, and personnel. This is especially true at the outset of an investigation. Under these circumstances, maintaining investigative secrecy is a formidable challenge. The crucial element of surprise is frequently lost.

Jurisdictional Challenges

Perhaps the most obvious implication of special prosecutors' limited jurisdiction is that they sometimes bump up against the limits of their authority. More often, defendants or witnesses in special prosecutor investigations unsuccessfully challenge the jurisdiction of the special prosecutor. This leads to delays while courts evaluate the merits of these challenges. The problem is worst when special prosecutors are authorized to investigate "any matters that may arise directly" from their original investigation. This flexible language reflects the reality that criminal investigations often lead in unexpected directions. But flexibility has costs as well as benefits. It gives special prosecutors more latitude, but it also gives opposing lawyers more ammunition for raising jurisdictional objections.

When veteran securities lawyer Alexia Morrison was appointed to investigate Justice Department lawyer Ted Olson, she ran into immediate difficulties. The terms of her appointment authorized Morrison to investigate whether Olson had lied to Congress. But she believed that Olson might have conspired with two other Justice Department officials to stymie a congressional investigation of the Environmental Protection Agency. She asked Attorney General Edwin Meese to extend her jurisdiction to cover the other officials. But he twice refused to do so, and the courts backed him up. Morrison would not be allowed to investigate the other officials, but she could investigate whether Olson had conspired with them to deceive Congress.

Based on this ruling, Morrison was ultimately permitted to subpoena the testimony of the other officials. But no ordinary federal prosecutor would have had to endure such delays and procedural wrangling to obtain a simple subpoena. This episode illustrates the power of the attorney general to place potentially important matters outside the special prosecutor's jurisdiction. It also illustrates the ability of witnesses and defendants to exploit ambiguity in that jurisdiction to delay a special prosecutor's investigation.

The experiences of special prosecutor Donald Smaltz illustrate the same point even more vividly. Smaltz's original assignment was to investigate whether Secretary of Agriculture Mike Espy had accepted illegal gifts. Smaltz's jurisdiction also encompassed any criminal activity "connected with or arising out of that investigation." Despite this broad grant of authority, Smaltz's investigation faced a "never-ending" stream of jurisdictional challenges. In just over a year, the authority of his office in grand jury matters— subpoenas to compel testimony, production of documents, and the like—was challenged forty-three separate times. Dozens more challenges followed in subsequent months and years.[8]

The predictable result was delay and inefficiency. It was not just that investigators were forced to wait for particular documents or testimony. The different components of an investigation are interconnected. "Where the ruling is not made promptly," Smaltz recalled, "the ability to conduct an orderly and deliberate investigation is destroyed. Without the documents, witness interviews are delayed. Agents and lawyers assigned to review the subpoenaed materials now must turn their attention and efforts elsewhere. When the documents are ultimately obtained, those agents who had the learning curve on this area may have become unavailable. Now, new agents and lawyers may have to be assigned to start from ground zero."[9]

A Singular Focus

More subtle but probably more important, the singular focus of special prosecutors can erode their sense of proportion. Ordinary federal prosecutors have a broad statutory responsibility to "prosecute for all offenses against the United States" within their districts. But there are far more crimes than any U.S. attorney's office could possibly prosecute. As a result, ordinary prosecutors are forced to consider which crimes are worth the expenditure of the office's limited resources. Investigating and prosecuting any one crime means leaving another uninvestigated and unprosecuted. Some of these trade-offs are made by senior Justice Department leadership as a matter of broad policy. Many, however, are left to the discretion of individual U.S. attorneys and their subordinates. For every case, ordinary prosecutors must ask themselves whether they can obtain a criminal conviction. But they must also ask whether bringing a criminal prosecution would serve the public interest. This sense of balance and proportion this fosters is a crucial counterweight to the competitive adversarial instincts that might otherwise drive prosecutors to excess.

The position of special prosecutors is very different. Like ordinary prosecutors, special prosecutors are bound by formal Justice Department policies that bar the prosecution of certain crimes under specified circumstances. But in a typical case, those policies are flexible enough to allow special prosecutors vast discretion. Unlike ordinary federal prosecutors, special prosecutors need not worry about the trade-offs that a decision to prosecute entails. Of course, those trade-offs still exist. The money spent on special prosecutor investigations and prosecutions would otherwise be available for other uses. But for special prosecutors, such opportunity costs are largely abstract. By proceeding with an investigation or prosecution, they will almost never limit their own options in another case.

As a result, special prosecutors can easily come to see their job as bringing any prosecution that the evidence will support. It does not help that special prosecutors are often elder statesman types, with little recent experience in the trenches of criminal prosecution. To live up to their own elevated reputations, it is easy to imagine how such figures might pursue their targets with a gusto bordering on monomania. As former Justice Department lawyer Mark Rasch observes, "they have one target, unlimited funds, and their job is to find any criminality they can. It's like an organized crime case: You don't say, 'Here's a crime, did Sammy the Bull do it?' You say, 'Sammy the Bull is an organized crime figure. Let's see what we can get on him.' "[10]

When Kenneth Starr was appointed to investigate Bill and Hillary Clinton's Whitewater land deal, he was a well-respected lawyer and former judge. When he resigned the position five years later, he was a tragic hero to a small hard core of the political right. To most of the broader public, he was a reviled and villainous figure. At the time of his resignation, nearly 70 percent of Americans viewed Starr unfavorably.[11] The conventional media narrative surrounding his sprawling investigation painted him as an obsessive, Ahab-like figure. Like the Clintons, most Americans saw Starr as a conservative zealot, committed to bringing down the president at any cost.

Ironically, as a judge years before, Starr himself had passed a similar verdict on special prosecutor Whitney Seymour, Jr. As Starr saw it, Seymour's prosecution of a Reagan White House aide evinced "a monomaniacal determination to get to the facts no matter what." Starr, not Seymour, became "the poster boy for all that was excessive and dangerous" about special prosecutors. Yet the harsh criticism of his investigation was far from exceptional.

Historically, the president's political allies have attacked the vast majority of special prosecutors in similar terms. The attacks were especially intense between 1978 and 1998, when judges rather than presidents appointed special prosecutors and had the power to veto their dismissal. But the attacks have been around as long as special prosecutors.[12]

This naturally raises the question: Does the narrow focus of special prosecutors actually encourage overzealousness and monomania? Or are caricatured portrayals of obsessive and unhinged special prosecutors mostly a weapon of political propaganda? The best answer probably lies somewhere in the middle.

Special prosecutors, no less than presidents, clearly can and sometimes do abuse their power. Kenneth Starr's investigation went awry in ways strongly suggestive of a warped sense of proportion. Yet special prosecutor investigations as a whole present a far more edifying picture. In modern times, most have ended without indictments, belying the inevitability of monomaniacal obsession.[13] Watergate special prosecutors Archibald Cox and Leon Jaworski played a vital role in bringing to light a "cancer on the presidency." Many less prominent special prosecutor investigations have also helped to root out lawbreaking in the executive branch. Overall, as political scientist Katy Harriger explains, most special prosecutors "have acted in ways that can be characterized as restrained and responsible."[14]

Finally, the threat of triggering a special prosecutor investigation—a sort of legal sword of Damocles hanging over the presidency—has probably deterred some lawbreaking among high executive officials. As legal scholar Cass Sunstein has observed of impeachment, "the value of the sword is not that it falls, but rather, that it hangs."[15] More precisely, the value of the sword is not *only* that it falls. There is also value in the mere threat of a special prosecutor investigation. But that threat will be credible only if it is actually carried out, at least occasionally.

Prosecuting in Public

The most important challenge special prosecutors face is that they must virtually always work under intense public scrutiny. It is usually public scrutiny that triggers the appointment of a special prosecutor in the first place. Even where that is not the case, the appointment of a special prosecutor nearly always makes headlines. By contrast, very few ordinary criminal investigations receive significant public attention before charges are filed. The upshot, as Donald Smaltz ruefully observes, is that special prosecutors are "from the outset, almost by definition, conducting a political investigation."[16]

On the one hand this makes the job of a special prosecutor far more difficult and complicated than that of an ordinary prosecutor. Special prosecutors face enormous political pressure to avoid even the appearance of partisan bias or political motivation. They are often subjected to vituperative and unfounded criticism by the president's political allies, which creates an atmosphere of constant threat. At any moment, the president may order them fired. He unquestionably has the power to do this, though he must act through the attorney general, who might complicate matters by resigning.

On the other hand the high visibility of special prosecutor investigations makes it more difficult for the president to fire them or otherwise cover up wrongdoing. The public is paying too much attention. Even a special prosecutor fired by the president can serve as a canary in the coal mine. The best example is Archibald Cox, whose firing by Richard Nixon triggered the resignation of both the attorney general and the deputy attorney general. The resulting public outcry forced Nixon to appoint another genuinely independent special prosecutor, whose investigation led directly to the end of Nixon's presidency. In sum, democratic politics is both the greatest challenge special prosecutors face and the greatest safeguard of their ability to protect the rule of law.

This double-edged relationship between politics and the rule of law is the central theme of the chapters that follow. If the American people tolerate presidential lawbreaking or complicity in the lawbreaking of others, no special prosecutor can save them. If the American people demand accountability and transparency, special prosecutors can serve as powerful, albeit fallible, guardians of the rule of law. The choice is ours.

PART I History

2

The First One Hundred Years

For many contemporary readers, the term special prosecutor is likely to call up Watergate, Kenneth Starr's investigation of Bill Clinton, and perhaps the Iran-Contra scandal. But those investigations grew out of a rich, complicated, and not always edifying history that even most legal scholars and historians have largely forgotten. Between 1875 and 1973, five different presidents appointed special prosecutors to investigate all manner of high-level official corruption. This chapter tells the stories of three such investigations, which provide crucial lessons for understanding modern-day special prosecutors.

These investigations span nearly a century, during which American society and governmental institutions underwent sweeping, transformational changes. Even so, these investigations share much in common. In each case, popular outcry over alleged misconduct by high executive officials forced the president to appoint a special prosecutor to restore public confidence. In each case, the high public salience of the resulting investigation gave the president's supporters powerful incentives to attack the special prosecutor. But the special prosecutor's visibility also provided the American people a potent tool for holding presidents accountable. In each case, the willingness and ability of the American people to impose a political price on the president proved decisive. Right from the beginning, politics was a double-edged sword for special prosecutors and their ability to safeguard the rule of law.

The St. Louis Whiskey Ring

On the morning of Saturday, February 12, 1876, an illustrious visitor arrived at the White House to perform an unusual duty. The visitor was chief justice of the United States Morrison Waite. The duty was to preside over the deposition of President Ulysses S. Grant. Never before or since has a sitting president testified on behalf of a defendant in a federal criminal prosecution. Grant's cabinet had unanimously counseled him against doing so. But his beloved chief of staff, Orville Babcock, was facing federal bribery charges in St. Louis, and Grant could not be dissuaded.[1]

Lieutenant General Ulysses Grant first won the presidency in 1868 as the conquering hero of Appomattox. Unfortunately, his military success little prepared him to deal with the wily operators of Washington. By the summer of 1875, the luster of his postwar reputation had dimmed considerably. A decent and honorable man himself, Grant proved a spectacularly bad judge of character in others, up to and past the point of gullibility. He was also legendarily stubborn in sticking by friends he appointed to high office, long after the evidence showed them to be corrupt or unfit for their duties. No episode more clearly exposed these faults than the notorious kickback conspiracy known as the St. Louis Whiskey Ring.[2]

The crux of the conspiracy was straightforward and brazen. Federal revenue agents in St. Louis and several other cities would look the other way while local distilleries dramatically underreported their whiskey production. This saved the distillery owners several million dollars in federal taxes, which were assessed per gallon of whiskey produced. In return, the distillery owners split the tax savings with federal officials. The local boss of this operation—the literal "ring-leader"—was General John McDonald, a rough-hewn former army comrade of President Grant. The real brains, however, belonged to General Orville Babcock, Grant's handsome, intelligent, and smoothly duplicitous protégé. While McDonald managed the scheme on the ground, the Iago-like Babcock ran interference in Washington, alerting McDonald to upcoming federal inspections by pseudonymous telegrams that Babcock poetically signed "Sylph."[3]

In the late spring of 1875, Babcock met his match in Benjamin Bristow, the secretary of the treasury. A zealous anticorruption crusader with presidential ambitions of his own, Bristow stealthily organized a series of dramatic, coordinated raids in force. This time, Babcock learned of the threat too late to warn his confederates. The criminal network Bristow uncovered was massive, as was the attendant scandal. Besides St. Louis, the Whiskey Ring encompassed Milwaukee, Cincinnati, New Orleans, and Peoria, Illinois. When Bristow presented Grant with the evidence he had gathered, including Babcock's telegrams, Grant appointed the first special prosecutor in U.S. history to investigate. "Let no guilty man escape," he directed.[4]

The historical record is disappointingly sparse on the circumstances surrounding this appointment and the considerations motivating it. This much is clear, however. Amid the burgeoning Whiskey Ring scandal, Grant removed William Patrick, the U.S. attorney for St. Louis, who was rumored to be intimate with several of the chief suspects. On May 20, 1875, Grant named former congressman David Dyer in Patrick's place. Dyer recommended that Grant appoint John B. Henderson, a former U.S. senator and Union general, as special prosecutor to head up the Whiskey Ring investigation.[5]

An accomplished St. Louis lawyer, Henderson enjoyed a hard-won reputation for staunch independence. In 1868, he had cast the deciding vote against impeachment of President Grant's widely loathed predecessor, Andrew Johnson. This act of political courage earned Henderson admiration as a man of principle but permanently extinguished his future in the Republican Party. In this respect, Henderson fits the typical profile of modern special prosecutors, who tend to be prominent elder statesmen with conspicuous reputations for political independence. Whether this profile played any significant role in Grant's decision is unknown. But his replacement of the St. Louis U.S. attorney and appointment of Henderson were unquestionably aimed at restoring public confidence in the integrity of federal law enforcement.[6]

The political and human drama could hardly have been higher. Just ten years after the Civil War, every significant player on both sides was a former Union general. This included Henderson and his principal antagonists, John McDonald and Orville Babcock. It also emphatically included Ulysses Grant, the former Union general-in-chief, who was not formally a party to the case but might as well have been. With such a clash of titans looming, all eyes fixed on the booming midwestern metropolis of St. Louis. Local newspapers proudly declared the proceedings "the most important trial ever held in the United States."[7]

McDonald was undeniably guilty, and a jury readily convicted him. The evidence against Babcock was nearly as damning, but Grant's chief of staff was a schemer of unusually insidious brilliance. He had managed to convince the president completely of his innocence. This saved him. Highly partisan attacks, which Babcock helped orchestrate, persuaded Grant that Henderson's investigation was a direct attack on the presidency. One typical Missouri correspondent wrote Grant that Henderson did not "like a bone in your body."[8] The final straw was Henderson's strident closing argument in the trial of Whiskey Ring conspirator William Avery. Caught up in his own eloquence, the special prosecutor imprudently hinted that Grant himself might have aided the conspirators. Outraged, the president fired Henderson just on the eve of Babcock's trial, scuttling many months of careful preparation.[9]

To his credit, Grant swiftly appointed another special prosecutor to succeed Henderson. But when the screws again tightened, the shameless Babcock appealed to Grant for help. Moved by his friend's plight and galled by the perceived assault on his administration, Grant agreed to testify in Babcock's defense. On the evening of February 9, 1876, Secretary of State Hamilton Fish recorded the event in his diary: "the President manifested a great deal of excitement and complained that they had taken from him his secretaries, and clerks, his messengers, and doorkeepers; that the prosecution was aimed at himself and that they were putting him on trial; that he was as confident as he lived of Babcock's innocence, and that he knew he was not guilty." Only Fish's fervent pleading dissuaded Grant from appearing at Babcock's trial in person.[10]

The deposition took place around a crowded table. Besides Chief Justice Waite and President Grant, the participants included lawyers Lucien Eaton, for the prosecution, and William A. Cook, for the defense. Hamilton Fish, Attorney General Edwards Pierrepont, and Treasury Secretary Benjamin Bristow all attended as witnesses. The grim-visaged chief justice began by placing Grant under oath. Eaton and Cook then took turns questioning the president about his knowledge of the Whiskey Ring and the allegations against Babcock.[11]

By 1876, Grant was a portlier and better-dressed version of his unassuming younger self. His sandy brown hair and beard had turned mostly gray. His eyes and mouth were even more careworn than in the Civil War portraits that made him famous around the world. Reflecting his increasingly antagonistic view of the prosecution, Grant answered many of Eaton's questions curtly or querulously. He professed little recollection of crucial details but vouched for Babcock's innocence emphatically and unequivocally. "I have always had great confidence in his integrity and his efficiency," Grant concluded. "And as yet my confidence in him is unshaken. I have never learned anything that would shake that confidence."[12]

Five days later, Babcock's defense attorney read the president's testimony aloud in a packed St. Louis courtroom. Judge, jury, and spectators listened with rapt attention. In the words of one eyewitness, all present "strained to catch the lightest accent" of Grant's words. The impact on the prosecution was nothing short of devastating. The jury acquitted Babcock after a mere two hours of deliberation.[13]

Despite this denouement, the Whiskey Ring investigation was not a total failure. Political pressure forced Grant to appoint Henderson, who convicted McDonald and dozens of lower level conspirators. This was a real advance in an era when graft and corruption were par for the course. On the other hand the political pressure that prompted Henderson's appointment was too weak to protect his investigation when it became irksome to the president. Grant paid no personal political price for scuttling the prosecution of Babcock, the most important and highly connected of the Whiskey Ring defendants. To the contrary, the partisan indignation of Grant's Republican supporters encouraged him in this course of action. A fractious but still robust Republican media apparatus amplified that indignation and broadcast it nationally. Party newspapers fed loyalists a sympathetic version of events while relentlessly attacking Henderson's motives and actions. In combination, these circumstances made it virtually inevitable that the double-edged sword of politics would fall on the special prosecutor, rather than the president.[14]

Teapot Dome

On November 30, 1921, two well-dressed young men walked into the lobby of the Wardman Park Hotel in northwest Washington, D.C. One of them carried a small black bag. Inside were five neatly wrapped stacks of bills, each containing $20,000. The man holding the bag was Ned Doheny, heir to one of the largest oil empires in the United States. By his side was Hugh Plunkett, Doheny's personal secretary, chauffeur, and rumored lover. Inside the hotel, Doheny and Plunkett were greeted by a tall, fierce-looking man of about sixty. With a piercing gaze and bushy white mustache, he bore a slight resemblance to Mark Twain. This was Albert Fall, President Warren Harding's secretary of the interior. Just two days earlier, Fall had agreed to award Ned's father, Edward Doheny, a federal oil lease worth hundreds of millions of dollars. There had been no other bidders.[15]

A former U.S. senator from New Mexico and a veteran of its cattle range wars, Fall was a living relic of the Wild West. As a frontier lawyer, he once defended the man accused of murdering Pat Garrett, the sheriff who shot Billy the Kid. In earlier days, Fall was said to have disarmed the famed outlaw John Wesley Hardin in a Texas saloon. Fall had also been credibly, though never definitively, implicated in the assassination of a rival Lincoln County lawyer, along with his eight-year-old son. Forceful, ambitious, and razorsharp in his youth, Fall was now a man in steep and visible decline. He had lost two adult children in the great flu epidemic three years earlier, including his favorite son. Their deaths had taken a severe toll on him, but the greatest ordeal of Fall's life was still to come.[16]

Ned Doheny handed Fall the bag. The older man opened it and counted the money. The $100,000 was all there. This was the precise amount Fall needed to purchase water access for his beloved Three Rivers Ranch in New Mexico. He scrawled out a promissory note for the "loan," handed it to Doheny, and sent the two young men on their way. Today, the $100,000 in the bag would be worth well over a million dollars. The oil lease Fall awarded Doheny for the Elk Hills naval oil reserve would be worth roughly four billion.

Four months later, another young man visited Fall at his Wardman Park residence, this time bearing nearly $200,000. The visitor was Mahlon T. Everhart, Fall's son-in-law. He had come straight from the private railroad car of oil baron Harry F. Sinclair, whose Sinclair gas stations still dot American highways. Just a month earlier, Fall had awarded Sinclair an oil lease even more valuable than the one he had given Edward Doheny. The biggest prize was Salt Creek of Wyoming, then the richest oilfield in the world. The lease also encompassed an adjacent and more memorably named federal oil reserve known as Teapot Dome. This time there was no pretense about a loan. The bonds were a payoff for the lease, pure and simple. Fall would later send Everhart to hit up Sinclair for at least another $100,000. He was not disappointed.[17]

Together, these transactions culminated the most audacious and far-reaching conspiracy in the history of American politics. The plot began with the nomination of Warren Harding to head the Republican ticket in 1920. Dozens of the most powerful politicians and businessmen of the age were directly or indirectly involved. Even today, the precise scope of the conspiracy remains uncertain. But this much is not in doubt: Harry Sinclair, Jake "the Oil King" Hamon, and others conspired to make Harding president. And they did so for one reason—to get their hands on federal oil reserves.[18]

Harding had one major strength. With his strong, handsome features, he "looked more like a president than any president who ever lived." But no one had much respect for his intellect. The real power in the administration would belong to Harry Daugherty,

Harding's wily, lazy-eyed campaign manager and later attorney general. And Daugherty was open for business. In exchange for a cool million dollars, he promised that Harding would name Jake Hamon secretary of the interior. In that capacity, Hamon would have free rein to plunder the federal oil lands he and his cronies had been salivating over. But there was a hitch. When Hamon attempted to abandon his longtime mistress to move to Washington, she shot him. He died five days later. Consequently, the job, and the dirty work, fell to Albert Fall.[19]

Initially, all went smoothly, but Fall made powerful enemies during his first year in office. They would ultimately prove his undoing. Harding's predecessor, Woodrow Wilson, had appointed committed conservationists to senior leadership positions in the Department of the Interior. Now they were on the outside looking in, and they did not like what they saw. One of these men, Henry Slattery, got wind of Sinclair's no-bid lease on Teapot Dome and leaked the story to the *Wall Street Journal*. It ran on the front page the next day. Soon other oilmen were raising questions. Why had they not been given a a chance at the action? Smelling blood, Slattery lobbied Progressive Senate gadfly "Fighting Bob" La Follette to push for an investigation..[20]

Now largely forgotten, Robert La Follette was once regarded as a great titan of the U.S. Senate. In 1959, a committee chaired by John F. Kennedy named him as one of the five "most outstanding" Senators in U.S. history. The committee praised La Follette as a "ceaseless battler for the underprivileged" and a "courageous independent." By 1922, Fighting Bob was nearing the end of his life, but he still had plenty of fire in his belly. The Teapot Dome lease violated two of his core principles: conservation and good government. On April 28, La Follette rose in the Senate chamber to denounce "the mystery, evasions, and denials that have emanated from the Interior Department for weeks." The next day, his resolution calling for a thorough investigation passed without opposition.[21]

Leadership of the investigation fell to Senator Thomas J. Walsh. A sixty-two-year-old Montana Democrat, Walsh was a formidable lawyer of erect bearing and penetrating blue eyes. His full head of silver hair and prominently peaked eyebrows gave him the appearance of a judge or a stern headmaster. He had not particularly wanted the job. But La Follette talked him into service, fearing that his Republican colleagues would sweep any scandal under the rug. He had picked the right man. Initially, Walsh was a somewhat reluctant inquisitor, but he gradually warmed to the task.

It took more than a year just to wade through the truckloads of documents provided by the Department of the Interior. Abandoned by his fellow committee members, Walsh completed the work almost entirely on his own. Most senators would have given up after a few months, but Walsh persevered. He convened his first hearings on October 23, 1923, more than a year after La Follette's original call for an investigation. But matters did not really begin to heat up until January 24, 1924.

On that date, Edward Doheny appeared before the Committee to answer questions about the lucrative oil lease Albert Fall had awarded him two years earlier. With practiced bonhomie, he began by embellishing his youthful acquaintance with Fall into a lifelong friendship. He then admitted to loaning the Secretary of the Interior $100,000 shortly before signing a lease for the Elk Hills oilfields. In his own previous testimony, Albert Fall had refused to disclose the source of these funds but adamantly denied that they had come from Doheny. The old tycoon's testimony made it immediately, painfully clear that Fall had lied to his former Senate colleagues. It also strongly suggested that the $100,000 "loan" had been a bribe. In one afternoon, Doheny had transformed Walsh's investigation from a sleepy backwater—one Senator literally fell asleep at the first hearing—into a national obsession.[22]

President Harding was not around to face the music. He had died of a heart attack the previous August, while the scandal was still in its infancy. As a result, "Teapot Dome" was now the problem of Harding's vice president and successor, Calvin Coolidge. Facing intense pressure to act, Coolidge did so swiftly and shrewdly. Rather than manning the barricades, he called for the appointment of two special prosecutors "of high rank drawn from both political parties." Congress immediately appropriated funds for such a team. But Coolidge's first two nominees were both forced to withdraw under fire over their close ties to the oil industry.

On February 2, 1924, Senator George Pepper of Pennsylvania, telephoned his former law student and friend Owen Roberts. Could Roberts meet him in Washington four days hence? Now a prominent Philadelphia attorney, Roberts said that he could. Tall, broad-shouldered, and solemn, Roberts had been teaching law at the University of Pennsylvania for twenty years, but he had no significant national reputation. When he arrived at Pepper's office, the senator informed him that they had an appointment with the president that afternoon.

A close confidant of Coolidge, Pepper had recommended that "Silent Cal" appoint Roberts as one of the two special prosecutors authorized by Congress. When Pepper and Roberts arrived at the White House, the president lived up to his nickname. After some extremely brief small talk about their respective farms, Coolidge asked Roberts one question about his knowledge of public lands law. Roberts answered that he knew very little but thought he could come up to speed. That was good enough for the president. Roberts got the nod. The other nominee was former Ohio Senator Atlee Pomerene, a Democrat. The Senate confirmed both by comfortable margins.[23]

Initially, Thomas Walsh worried that the little-known Roberts would serve as a cat's paw for Coolidge. If true, this could sap the Senate investigation of its momentum while allowing the White House to create the appearance of a vigorous response. Walsh was mistaken. Roberts, who would later be named to the U.S. Supreme Court by President Herbert Hoover, proved a dogged and capable special prosecutor. He was a far better lawyer than Atlee Pomerene and quickly took the lead in their joint investigation.[24]

Somewhat unusually for special prosecutors, Roberts and Pomerene were empowered to bring both civil and criminal actions as necessary. Their first and probably most important move was to file civil suits to cancel the Doheny and Sinclair oil leases. Both were ultimately successful, though Roberts and Pomerene lost the Sinclair case at the trial court. Afterward, the unsympathetic Wyoming judge promptly departed for the Mediterranean on Harry Sinclair's yacht. This decision was reversed on appeal, and the Supreme Court affirmed. As a result, both leases were canceled, and hundreds of millions in oil wealth was returned to the American people.[25]

Roberts and Pomerene also brought eight criminal cases but obtained only two convictions after many years of delays. On October 26, 1929, a seriously ill and wheelchair-bound Albert Fall was convicted of taking a bribe from Edward Doheny. Harry Sinclair was convicted of jury tampering on February 21, 1928. Both spent less than a year in jail. In an ironic twist, Doheny was acquitted of offering the same bribe that Fall was convicted of taking.

Nevertheless, Doheny paid a devastating price. His son Ned was also charged with bribery for his role in delivering the $100,000 to Fall. On the eve of their scheduled trial, Ned died in a grisly murder-suicide at his opulent Beverly Hills estate. He was thirty-six. The other victim was his personal secretary, Hugh Plunckett, who had accompanied him to deliver the $100,000 to Albert Fall. Unlike the Dohenys, Plunckett had not been charged with any crime. But he would have been a key witness at the bribery trial.

A hurried inquest declared Ned Doheny the murder victim and Plunkett the suicide, though much of the physical evidence suggested the contrary. The elder Doheny subsequently foreclosed on the property Fall had purchased with the infamous "loan." On top of his other misfortunes, this reduced the former secretary of the interior to a charity case for the remainder of his life.[26]

Like the Whiskey Ring scandal, Teapot Dome left a mixed legacy. On the one hand political pressure forced the appointment of two genuinely independent special prosecutors. That pressure endured long enough to sustain the special prosecutors in their civil suits to cancel the Doheny and Sinclair leases. It also sustained their successful prosecutions of Albert Fall for bribery and Harry Sinclair for criminal contempt. These convictions showed "that justice, even when leaden-footed, at last overtakes the criminal"— at least sometimes. Albert Fall's sorry fate may well have "put fear in the hearts" of at least some "public officials tempted to betray their trust." A popular myth even credits Fall as the inspiration for the expressions "taking the fall" and "fall guy," but this is probably apocryphal.[27]

On the other hand, most of the public officials who betrayed the public trust in this saga did not face any serious reckoning. The same goes for most of the private citizens who aided and abetted that betrayal. One important reason for this was the 1924 election. The President and his congressional allies had actively undermined the Teapot Dome investigations. But voters overwhelmingly chose to return Calvin Coolidge to the presidency and Republican majorities to both houses of Congress. Those majorities repeatedly dragged their feet in appropriating funds, actually forcing the special prosecutors to fund the investigation out of their own pockets.

As Felix Frankfurter, a Harvard law professor and later Supreme Court justice, summed it up in the *New Republic*, "governmental machinery, prestige, wealth, and agencies of publicity—all were for covering things up."[28] No special prosecutor could hope to hold the president and his close associates fully accountable under such circumstances.

The Truman Tax Scandals

Uncharismatic, lacking in polish, and a poor public speaker, Harry S. Truman might easily have spent his entire career as a minor county official in Kansas City, Missouri. But in 1934, four other more promising candidates declined to run for the U.S. Senate. Lacking a better option, the notoriously corrupt political boss Thomas Pendergast threw his formidable weight behind Truman. Fifty years old, with a checkered business career and little prior political experience, Truman was hardly an obvious choice for high office. But Pendergast's hold over Missouri politics was at its zenith, and Truman narrowly edged out his two principal rivals for the Democratic nomination. That was the ball game. In a harbinger of Franklin Roosevelt's 1936 landslide, Truman defeated his Republican general election opponent by more than twenty points.[29]

Despite his roots in the bare-knuckle world of urban machine politics, Truman ultimately made his name as a good-government crusader. Just six years into his Senate career, he deftly secured the job of leading a new Special Committee to Investigate the National Defense Program. To Truman's lasting benefit, this cumbersome name was quickly replaced by a shorthand—"the Truman Committee."

With World War II raging, any hint of mismanagement in the nation's war mobilization was major news. Almost immediately,

Truman's dogged investigation of corruption, graft, and greed in military procurement grabbed headlines. In 1943, he appeared on the cover of *Time*, looking earnestly into the distance, his brow heavily furrowed. The admiring caption read "Investigator Truman. A Democracy Has to Keep an Eye on Itself."

Truman's reputation as a principled watchdog of democracy put him into serious contention for the 1944 Democratic vice-presidential nomination. His deft political instincts and plainspoken populist style sealed the deal. He had served as vice president for just eighty-five days when Franklin Roosevelt's death from a brain hemorrhage vaulted him to the presidency on April 12, 1945.[30]

It was a short apprenticeship for the world's most demanding job. And it could hardly have come at a more crucial juncture in world history. Truman's eight-year presidency spanned the end of World War II, the dawn of the Cold War, most of the Korean War, and the rise of McCarthyism at home. It also spanned a crucial period in the evolution of American domestic politics away from the patronage system that had dominated the nineteenth century. In the heyday of the old system, it was generally understood that "some impropriety and petty graft were part of the process of government." This was "messy and distasteful, perhaps, but unavoidable." Norms, however, were changing fast. As a creature of the old system, Truman found himself caught in the middle.[31]

By the final year of his final term of office, rumors of corruption in Truman's administration were swirling thickly. The bulk of suspicion centered on the Justice Department and the Bureau of Internal Revenue, the predecessor of the Internal Revenue Service. Federal revenue collections had increased eightfold during World War II. The enormous expansion of the bureaucracy this required, virtually overnight, all but guaranteed that some bad apples would make it into the barrel. Now the bill was coming due. In 1951 alone, dozens of mostly low-level officials were forced to resign over allegations of bribery, extortion, and embezzlement. In a typical case, a small business owner or lawyer who owed back taxes would be subtly—and sometimes unsubtly—shaken down for bribes and other favors. Many of the officials involved were subsequently convicted and sent to prison.

"The cumulative impression," as one Truman biographer describes it, "was of a tax bureaucracy rotten through and through, a president lax and complacent." By the end of 1951, the cloud of scandal had expanded to encompass nearly a dozen federal agencies. Exploiting the controversy, an ambitious junior senator from California proposed that federal grand juries be allowed to appoint special prosecutors on their own authority. His name was Richard Nixon. Nothing came of this, but under mounting pressure, Truman announced that his attorney general, Howard McGrath, would lead an inquiry.[32]

The public outcry was quick and forceful. As head of one of the departments to be investigated, the handsome, hard-drinking McGrath was hardly a disinterested party. In the eyes of many, he was part of the problem that needed investigating. Neither Congress nor the public trusted him to conduct a vigorous and impartial inquiry. To quiet the furor, Truman quickly acquiesced to the appointment of an outside special prosecutor. Following the advice of legendary federal judge Learned Hand, McGrath tapped a reform-minded New York lawyer named Newbold Morris for the job.

Cocksure and remarkably tone-deaf in personal interactions, Morris was an experienced lawyer but a neophyte in the ways of Washington. His investigation ran into obstacles right from the start. After a bizarre power struggle in Congress, he was denied the authority to issue subpoenas. Publicly, Morris declared that he did not need it because Truman had promised him full cooperation. If every executive employee voluntarily turned over documents and submitted to questioning, Morris would have no need to resort to judicial orders. But Attorney General McGrath had other ideas. Matters came to a head when Morris demanded that McGrath turn over detailed information about his own activities and personal finances. The Attorney General refused to comply and summarily dismissed Morris, who had held office for just two months. Hours later, Truman fired McGrath. The reasons for this decision remain unclear. Truman may have been displeased with the firing of Morris or simply with how McGrath carried out this decision.[33] Truman's later comments suggest that McGrath had become too much of a political liability to be kept on.[34]

Compared to the St. Louis Whiskey Ring and Teapot Dome, the Truman tax scandals were remarkably small-bore—"piddling" even, to quote one Truman biographer. Even so, they teach a remarkably similar lesson about the relationship between special prosecutors and democratic politics.

On the one hand political pressure forced Truman to appoint a genuinely independent special prosecutor to investigate his own Justice Department. That special prosecutor was fired before completing his investigation. But his dismissal immediately led Truman to fire Attorney General McGrath, who headed the scandal-ridden department. Asked to reflect on his investigation, Newbold Morris reportedly remarked: "If I got rid of nothing else, I got rid of Howard McGrath."[35]

On the other hand Truman was a lame duck when these scandals arose. As a result, he never seems to have felt any real pressure to get to the bottom of the matter. A subsequent congressional investigation concluded that Morris's experiences were "replete with indications of bad faith toward his work on the part of his superiors." Truman's firing of McGrath was at best a partial response. It also short-circuited any serious further investigation.[36]

As with the Whiskey Ring and Teapot Dome scandals, the lesson is clear. When a president no longer feels political pressure to support an independent investigation, a special prosecutor can do little of importance. In such circumstances, special prosecutors may be rendered ineffectual even with the support of the American people. Without that support, their failure is virtually inevitable.

3

A Cancer on the Presidency

On the afternoon of Saturday, October 20, 1973, Watergate special prosecutor Archibald Cox walked into the National Press Club with his wife, Phyllis. The two posed for photos in front of an American flag before Cox took his seat on the stage alone. As they parted, each gave the other's hand a poignant squeeze.

Seated before a long table, Cox wore a gray suit, a maroon striped tie, and a nervous smile. Hundreds of reporters hunched over notepads packed the gallery. In living rooms across the country, millions of Americans watched the live television broadcast on tenterhooks. The previous night President Richard Nixon had made a shocking announcement. He would defy a court order to turn over tape recordings of his private White House meetings. A constitutional crisis was in progress. How would the special prosecutor respond?[1]

A Harvard law professor and former solicitor general of the United States, Cox had taken up his post as special prosecutor just five months earlier. His principal charge was to investigate the cover-up of a botched burglary by Nixon campaign operatives on June 17, 1972. The burglars' target was the Democratic National Committee headquarters at the Watergate office complex. The name "Watergate" quickly became shorthand for a host of alleged misconduct by the president's 1972 reelection campaign. Archibald Cox was authorized to investigate all of it.[2]

The appointment of Cox, a widely respected Democrat, helped President Nixon to signal that he was serious about investigating the misdeeds of his campaign staff. But the relationship quickly became contentious and adversarial. The final straw was Cox's insistence on seeking access to the White House tapes. Facing a court order to turn them over, the president instructed Cox, "as an employee of the executive branch," to stand down.[3]

Gray-haired and beetle-browed, Cox bent to the microphone on the table before him. He began by apologizing for bringing the assembled reporters out on such a lovely fall afternoon. He then methodically laid out his case for seeking the tapes. American institutions were at stake, he explained. As special prosecutor, he had to do what he felt was right. This was what he had promised the U.S. Senate when he was appointed. At the very same Senate hearing, Attorney General Elliott Richardson had promised that Cox would be allowed to do his job without White House inter-ference. Richardson also promised that Cox could be fired only for "extraordinary improprieties." Of course, Cox conceded, "a President can always work his will." But he would not allow him-self to be swayed by that possibility.[4]

To most Americans, Cox came across as dignified, principled, and humble in the face of awesome responsibility. Predictably, a paranoid and embittered Richard Nixon viewed Cox's performance differently. Instead of courage and conscience, Nixon saw defiant grandstanding and rank insubordination. This was the final straw. He gave the order to fire Cox, which his chief of staff, Alexander Haig, relayed to Attorney General Richardson by phone. An in-creasingly disgusted Richardson had seen this coming for several days. He joined the administration to serve his country but now felt he had been cruelly used, his spotless reputation dragged through the mud. There was little question in his mind what he had to do. Over Haig's vain protests, Richardson demanded a personal meeting with the president. He delivered his resignation at 4:30 that afternoon.[5]

This made Deputy Attorney General William Ruckelshaus, formerly the first head of the Environmental Protection Agency, the acting attorney general. But Ruckelshaus, too, resigned rather than fire Cox. Finally, Nixon found his man in Solicitor General Robert Bork. The bushy-haired future Supreme Court nominee promptly dispatched a letter by personal messenger notifying Cox of his dismissal. Within days, this episode became known as "the Saturday Night Massacre.[6]"

Things Fall Apart

Nineteen seventy-three was a whirlwind year. Internationally, the two most significant events were the signing of the Paris Peace Accords on January 14 and the Yom Kippur War, which began on October 6. The Paris Peace Accords formally ended the Vietnam War. The Yom Kippur War began with a massive Egyptian attack on Israeli military positions along the Suez Canal. It ended with a decisive Israeli victory, after heavy casualties on both sides. In the spring and summer months separating these momentous events, the presidency of Richard Nixon began to unravel.

The first key development took place on March 19. On that date, Watergate burglar and former CIA officer James McCord delivered a typewritten letter to federal district judge John Sirica. In stilted and circumlocutory prose, the letter alleged that "there was political pressure applied to the defendants to plead guilty and remain silent." If true, this would probably constitute a federal crime— obstruction of justice, suborning of perjury, witness tampering, or perhaps all three. These are serious offenses, which can result in significant prison time. If they were committed by persons close to the president, that would constitute a national scandal of potentially enormous proportions. If the president himself participated in the conspiracy, it might even mean impeachment, though that possibility still seemed remote at this stage.[7]

A gruff former professional boxer, Judge Sirica had long suspected a cover-up. All of the accused burglars, however, had denied under oath that any senior officials had participated in orchestrating the Watergate break-in. The whole operation, they said, had been the brainchild of Howard Hunt and Gordon Liddy, two low-level officials in Nixon's 1972 presidential campaign. Now, in McCord's letter, the judge had his smoking gun. Alluding to possible threats against McCord's life and family, the letter was frustratingly short on specifics. But it clearly stated that "others involved in the Watergate operation were not identified at trial, when they could have been by those testifying.[8]"

The Watergate burglars were scheduled for sentencing on March 23. This gave the judge a captive audience, and he would not waste it. After the initial buzz of the crowd died down, Sirica began the proceedings with wry understatement. There was a small preliminary matter, he said, that the court needed to deal with before the sentencing. He then read McCord's letter aloud, in its entirety, for the record. In the audience, at Sirica's invitation, was an unassuming Georgetown law professor named Sam Dash. In a few months, Dash's name and face—and signature dark-framed glasses—would become a fixture on front pages and television screens. But for the moment, the newly named chief counsel to the Senate Watergate Committee could walk into a courtroom without being noticed. He would always be glad that he had done so on this morning. McCord's letter was just the break his committee had been waiting for. With Judge Sirica's encouragement,

James McCord would shortly become the cooperating witness of Dash's dreams.[9]

After an initial interview with Dash, McCord agreed to testify before a secret session of the Senate Watergate Committee on March 29. The substance of this testimony leaked to the press, which reported that McCord had implicated higher-ups in the White House and the Nixon presidential campaign. The list of alleged conspirators was a veritable who's who of Nixon's inner circle. It included former attorney general John Mitchell, White House counsel John W. Dean III, and possibly White House chief of staff Bob Haldeman.

According to news reports, McCord described Mitchell as the "overall boss," of the Watergate operation and said that Dean had personally approved the burglary and bugging. An earlier *Los Angeles Times* story, anonymously planted by McCord, had also implicated Jeb Stuart Magruder, deputy director of the Nixon campaign. The week after McCord's testimony, both Dean and Magruder secretly—and separately—approached U.S. attorney Earl Silbert, offering their cooperation.[10]

From this point, things went downhill fast for the administration. At 1 a.m. on Sunday, April 15, Assistant Attorney General Henry Petersen called Attorney General Richard Kleindienst at home. Despite the hour, Petersen said, they had to speak urgently. He had just learned some earth-shaking news from Silbert. John Dean was prepared to implicate the president's two closest aides, Bob Haldeman and chief domestic advisor John Ehrlichman, in the Watergate cover-up.

After the president, Haldeman and Ehrlichman might have been the two most powerful men in Washington. Former classmates at UCLA, they had both been instrumental to Nixon's 1968 political rebirth. They were now the two pillars around which Nixon's entire White House operation was built. When Petersen arrived at

Kleindienst's house with Earl Silbert and his assistant Seymour Glanzer, Kleindienst was crying. The four men sat up talking about the case until 5 a.m. When the meeting broke up, Kleindienst cried again.[11]

By the end of the month, Haldeman, Ehrlichman, Dean, and Kleindienst would all be forced to resign. When the scandal first broke, Nixon's White House team plotted to "throw John Dean to the wolves" to save Haldeman and Ehrlichman. Over the next few weeks, a fast-moving game of cat and mouse played out in Oval Office meetings, frenzied negotiations with prosecutors, and strategic leaks to the press. In the end, the shrewd and slippery Dean consistently outmaneuvered the president's top aides. He was just thirty-five.

Ultimately, press reports of hush-money payments and deliberate destruction of evidence proved too damaging for Haldeman and Ehrlichman to survive. Meanwhile, Kleindienst recused himself from the Watergate matter, due to his close acquaintance with those under investigation. This put Henry Petersen in charge and diminished Kleindienst's usefulness to the president. For his part, the duplicitous Dean was finally and definitively recognized as a turncoat—an "asp in our bosom," in the words of one Nixon advisor. To maximally impress the public, Nixon decided that all four should go at once.[12]

The president announced the departures in a nationally televised speech on April 30, his first to address Watergate. "I want to talk to you from my heart," he began. He went on to describe the burglary and bugging as a "senseless illegal action." He expressed shock that "employees of the Re-Election Committee were apparently among the guilty." He then acknowledged, for the first time, that White House employees might have participated in "an effort to conceal the facts." He concluded by announcing the nomination of Elliot Richardson, "a man of unimpeachable integrity and rigorously high principle," to replace Kleindienst as attorney general. Richardson, Nixon emphasized, would have "absolute authority to make all decisions bearing upon the prosecution of the Watergate case and related matters." Almost as a footnote, Nixon mentioned that this authority would include the power to name a special prosecutor, if Richardson should deem that necessary.[13]

Why did Nixon take these dramatic steps? Forcing the resignations of Haldeman and Ehrlichman caused Nixon great personal anguish. In a meeting with Ehrlichman the day before his speech, he broke down weeping for several minutes. "It's like cutting off my arms," he wailed, with characteristic self-pity. In the weeks before the speech, he had categorically rejected Kleindienst's advice to appoint a special prosecutor. What had changed? The answer is simple. Political pressure to signal his seriousness about "this whole sordid affair" had grown too great to withstand. Nixon's previously sky-high poll numbers were dropping sharply. To restore public confidence, he had to take drastic action. Even that might not be enough.[14]

A New Sheriff in Town

On May 16, Elliott Richardson placed a call to an office at the University of California, Berkeley. On the other end of the line was Richardson's old mentor and labor law professor at Harvard, Archibald Cox. "Happy Birthday," Richardson said. Cox would turn sixty-one the following day. He was in Berkeley to deliver a series of lectures on the Supreme Court, and Richardson's call caught him quite by surprise. So did the fact that Richardson knew it was his birthday. The two men had crossed paths occasionally over the years, both in Washington and Boston, but they were far from intimate. Of course, Cox knew that Richardson had been nominated to succeed Richard Kleindienst as attorney general. But his knowledge of the situation in Washington went no further than what he read in the newspapers. Cox had not remained especially plugged in after leaving his post as solicitor general in 1965.

Richardson cut right to the point. He was calling to see if Cox would serve as Watergate special prosecutor. In many ways, Cox was an odd choice for the job. He had no substantial experience as a prosecutor or defense attorney—or even as a trial lawyer On the other hand he was a figure of real stature in the legal profession. Both Democrats and Republicans thought highly of him, and he had a strong reputation for independence. Besides, the first seven candidates Richardson approached had turned him down. He knew that Senate Democrats would refuse to confirm him as attorney general until he named a credible special prosecutor, and he was running out of choices. Richardson aide J. T. Smith put it baldly: "we were getting desperate.[15]"

Cox did not know this full background, but he was aware that other prominent lawyers had turned down the job. He therefore responded to Richardson's offer cautiously, even warily, though also with real interest. He pressed Richardson on the exact parameters of the role and what guarantees of independence he could offer. They agreed to speak further after Cox reviewed the draft guidelines drawn up by Richardson's assistant.

Over the next two days, Cox and Richardson spoke by telephone several more times, reaching agreement on three key points. First, if Cox took the job, he could be fired only for "extraordinary improprieties." Second, Cox would formally report to the attorney general, but he would have wide discretion in determining what information to share about his investigation. Richardson also agreed not to countermand or interfere with Cox's prosecutorial decisions. Finally, Cox would have jurisdiction to investigate not just the Watergate burglary and cover-up but "all offenses arising out of the 1972 presidential election." On the evening of May 17,

Cox took an overnight flight back to Boston, so he could talk things over with his wife. On May 18, he called Richardson to accept.[16]

Meanwhile, Nixon's April 30 speech had done nothing to arrest the accelerating pace of the scandal. On May 10, Nixon's poll numbers sunk into negative territory for the first time. Only 44 percent of Americans rated him favorably, while 45 percent rated him unfavorably. On May 18, the very afternoon that Elliott Richardson announced Cox's appointment as special prosecutor, James McCord offered shocking testimony before the Senate. In exchange for his silence about the Watergate burglary, McCord said, he had been promised executive clemency. This promise, he told senators, came "from the very highest levels of the White House." McCord's testimony marked the opening of the Senate Watergate Committee's live televised hearings, which transfixed the nation through early August.[17]

Thanks to these developments, Elliott Richardson's nomination faced real skepticism from Senate Democrats, who enjoyed a small but comfortable majority in that chamber. How, the senators wondered, could a special prosecutor supervised by the attorney general exercise genuine independence? What guarantees could Richardson provide that Cox would be not be pressured to divulge confidential information about his work? Despite intense pressure, Richardson refused to disclaim his supervisory power over the special prosecutor. That power, he said, was essential to the attorney general's role. Nevertheless, he insisted that Cox would be allowed to work independently.

When Democratic Senators were not reassured, Richardson brought Cox himself along to the hearings to explain his understanding of their arrangement. In a bravura performance, Cox promised to follow the investigative trail "wherever it may lead," even to the Oval Office. "I will have the whip hand," he said and insisted that he would not hesitate to use it. What would he do if

Richardson asked him to do anything improper? Cox said he would tell him: "the only way to exercise your final statutory authority is to fire me. It's your move."

Meanwhile, President Nixon offered his own assurances that Cox's appointment had his "full support." He also promised not to invoke executive privilege as to "any testimony concerning possible criminal conduct." In other words, Cox would have access to all evidence. This was enough to get Richardson confirmed. He and Cox both took the oath of office on May 26.[18]

A Long, Hot Summer

Cox had his work cut out for him. His broad jurisdiction over all crimes arising out of the 1972 election was both a blessing and a curse. It ensured that he would not have to fight with Richardson about the limits of his power. But the range of potential issues within his authority was staggering. It was difficult to know where to start.

Cox spent most of the month of June staffing his team. He soon realized that it would be helpful to subdivide the office into several separate "task forces." Each would take charge of investigating one cluster of alleged crimes. The list included bribery, political dirty tricks, campaign finance violations, and illegal surveillance. The main Watergate Task Force, consisting of eight mostly Ivy League lawyers, would investigate the burglary and alleged cover-up. Their average age was just thirty-one, though most had substantial prosecutorial experience.[19]

It was mid-June before Cox's team moved into its permanent offices at 1425 K Street NW. The delay was attributable mostly to the time required to install adequate security against eavesdropping. Cox would take no chances that his investigation of illegal surveillance would itself be illegally surveilled. When the lawyers and staff finally moved in, the office was protected around the clock by an impressive security apparatus. This included three armed guards and a supersensitive state-of-the-art alarm system. Cox even had special devices embedded in all the exterior walls to guard against "spike-mikes," a powerful type of surveillance microphone used by the FBI.[20]

This physical security was impressive, but it could not protect the special prosecutor's office against the greatest threat it confronted. Almost from the outset, Nixon and his political allies bombarded Cox with savage political attacks on his motives and conduct. It did not help that Cox had invited nine members of the Kennedy family, including Senator Ted Kennedy, to his swearing-in. This was like waving a red flag before a bull. As one of the president's lawyers put it, "the porcupine has flung all of its quills into the President's face."

Ever since his agonizingly narrow loss to John F. Kennedy in the 1960 presidential election, Nixon had nursed a seething, envy-tinged hatred for the entire Kennedy clan. Cox's public association with them, openly flaunted and widely reported in the press, had strongly reinforced Nixon's already formidable persecution complex. As if he did not have enough to worry about, his new attorney general had invited a true-blue Kennedy man right into the heart of Nixon's administration.[21]

The public attacks on Cox followed in short order. "White House propagandists put out the word," two young members of the Watergate task force remembered later. "Cox had assembled a staff of left-wing Democratic zealots jealous of the President's electoral victories, ideologically biased against his policies, and personally determined to 'get' him." This was not just a whispering campaign. It was a carefully orchestrated, comprehensive, and relentlessly pursued public relations strategy: "the White House was selling 'Watergate as vendetta' full time, and a lot of people were buying it."[22]

These attacks were baseless. As Elliott Richardson's aides concluded in vetting him, Cox was "nonpartisan almost to the point of prickliness." The team of lawyers he hired was politically diverse. It included several Republicans and at least one Democrat who had voted for Nixon in 1972, but most were basically apolitical. They were there not to push an ideological agenda but for the "sense of destiny" and "unprecedented responsibility"—in short, to participate in history.[23]

From a strategic standpoint, however, the attacks made perfect sense. Political pressure had forced Nixon to acquiesce in the appointment of a special prosecutor to signal he had nothing to hide. Now that he had done so, Cox's investigation clearly represented a serious threat to his presidency. Nixon had every incentive to undermine the special prosecutor's credibility. The best way to do that was to paint Cox as an ax-grinding zealot, leading a cabal of like-minded ideological crusaders. If enough people came to believe that, the public would likely perceive the fruits of Cox's investigation as tainted. The president might even get away with firing the special prosecutor. In fact, Nixon had begun to consider this possibility within just a few weeks of Cox's appointment. Would the American people take the bait? The answer to this question would make or break the special prosecutor's investigation.[24]

Meanwhile, the Senate Watergate hearings continued to captivate the nation. Now televised "gavel to gavel" on all three major networks, the hearings made a celebrity of the committee's septuagenarian chairman, North Carolina Democrat Sam Ervin. An ardent segregationist, Ervin had coauthored the Southern Manifesto protesting *Brown v. Board of Education*. Now, before the cameras, he styled himself as a simple country lawyer. Speaking in a rich Carolina drawl, he quoted the Bible and spun colorful yarns that delighted television viewers. During one exchange with a recalcitrant witness, Ervin retorted: "the President seems to extend executive privilege way out past the atmosphere. What he says is executive privilege is nothing but executive poppycock." Speaking of the president, he quoted Mark Twain, saying "the truth is precious; use it sparingly." Pausing for a beat, Ervin added, "Nixon used it sparingly."[25]

Ervin provided color and occasional comic relief. He was also a deceptively agile lawyer. But it was the witnesses that kept millions of Americans watching, none more so than John Dean. A slight man with precisely parted brown hair, the former White House counsel looked nervous when he entered the grand expanse of the Senate Caucus Room. The date was June 25, and he carried with him a 245-page opening statement. For the better part of two days, Dean read that statement to the committee in a somber, monotone voice. On page after page, he recounted President Nixon's enthusiastic encouragement of the Watergate cover-up. The accumulation of precise dates and other supporting details, drawn from Dean's contemporaneous notes, was extraordinary. After he finished, committee members questioned him for another two days but did little to undercut his dazzlingly vivid account.[26]

In one famous exchange, Tennessee senator Howard Baker demanded: "What did the President know and when did he know it?" This pithy and apparently hard-hitting question is often remembered as an example of investigatory zeal par excellence. But in context, Baker was clearly seeking to exonerate the president. If Nixon had only learned about the burglary and cover-up after the fact, he could not be guilty of directing or even participating in it. Dean's response was devastating. He and Nixon had discussed the cover-up thirty-five times. The earliest was on September 15, 1972, just two months after the burglary and well before Nixon claimed to have learned of the cover-up. This effectively silenced Baker.[27]

Dean's testimony changed everything. Other witnesses had hinted at Nixon's personal involvement in the cover-up, but Dean was the first to make such an allegation explicitly. Unlike other witnesses, he also had clear firsthand knowledge of the president's actions. For the first time, Nixon himself appeared to be in dire legal and political jeopardy.

A month before Dean's Senate appearance, Nixon had made a second major speech on Watergate. Apparently intended to be his final statement on the subject, the speech made seven distinct points, designed to preempt or refute the charges against him. Dean's testimony contradicted nearly all of them. It also went far beyond what he had previously told the U.S. attorney's office. Cox and his team now had to take much more seriously the possibility that the president of the United States had committed serious crimes. They also had to figure out whether Dean, who had demonstrated considerable ethical flexibility in the past, was finally telling the truth.[28]

Prelude to a Massacre

A method for answering this question presented itself sooner than Cox or anyone else could have hoped. Alexander Butterfield was a decorated Air Force pilot who flew ninety-eight combat missions in Vietnam. He was also a UCLA classmate of Bob Haldeman and John Ehrlichman. When Butterfield learned that Haldeman would be serving as Nixon's chief of staff, he had reached out to his old friend. Maybe there was a job for him? Butterfield had previously worked as an aide to the secretary of defense, a job that required him to spend a lot of time in the White House. On the strength of that experience, Haldeman hired him as deputy assistant to the president. In this capacity, Butterfield was responsible for the president's daily schedule, which is why Senate investigators initially called him in for an interview on July 13.[29]

They learned about something far more important than Nixon's appointments. For the past two months, both prosecutors and the Senate committee had suspected that some of Nixon's conversations were recorded. John Dean raised this possibility again in his Senate testimony, but he was only speculating. Finally, in a closed session before Butterfield's public testimony, a lawyer for Senate Republicans asked him point blank. Did the White House have any kind of recording system?

"I was wondering if someone would ask that," Butterfield replied. "There is tape in the Oval Office."

In fact, on February 10, 1971, Haldeman had asked Butterfield to supervise the installation of a secret, voice-activated taping system. No one, therefore, was more familiar with the technical details than Butterfield. He explained all this to the committee, right down to the location of the hidden microphones. He also added that "*everything* was taped as long as the President was in attendance. There was not so much as a hint that something should not be taped."[30]

The significance of Butterfield's revelations escaped no one. It was no longer a case of Dean's word against the president's. There was an objective record. Cox wasted no time. On July 18, two days after Butterfield publicly disclosed the president's recording system, the special prosecutor wrote the White House. He wanted to hear the tapes—eight in particular, whose dates and times he precisely indicated. This was no less than Cox felt he had been promised at the outset, full cooperation and no assertion of executive privilege.[31]

On July 23, in a letter drafted by lawyer Charles Alan Wright, Nixon bluntly refused Cox's request: "it will not be possible to make available to you the recordings that you have requested." Already a "colossus in the legal profession," as Justice Ruth

Bader Ginsburg would later describe him, Wright was not above throwing his weight around. On this occasion, he could not resist the opportunity to lecture his fellow constitutional law professor Cox. "Questions of separation of powers," Wright wrote, "are in the forefront when the most confidential documents of the presidency are sought for use in the Judicial Branch." Wright acknowledged that the president had supported the disclosure of certain materials, but he insisted that was not a blanket policy. "It is for the President, and only for the President, to weigh whether the incremental advantage that these tapes would give you in criminal proceedings justifies the serious and lasting hurt that disclosure would do to the effective functioning of the Presidency."[32]

Wright's letter left Cox no choice. He would have to seek a *subpoena duces tecum*—in plain English, a judicial order requiring the president to produce the tapes. The momentousness of this course was obvious to everyone involved. A sitting president had only been subpoenaed once before. On trial for treason, vice president Aaron Burr had sought to compel Thomas Jefferson to produce two letters written by Burr's alleged coconspirator. That complicated episode had ended ambiguously. Jefferson ultimately produced the letters Burr sought, with deletions to protect innocent third parties. Nixon would later cite this episode as a precedent for his own refusal to submit to a subpoena. But it is not at all clear that Jefferson actually defied any court order. To the contrary, he seems to have done just what the court asked of him. Still, Cox and his team knew they were taking a dramatic, well-nigh unprecedented step.[33]

There was also a more mundane issue. What should a subpoena to the president look like? Normally, issuing a subpoena is a pro forma exercise, in the literal sense that it is done using a boilerplate form. But there was no such form drafted for use against the president. Forced to improvise, Cox's team went with a bare-bones document directed to Richard M. Nixon or "any subordinate officer, official or employee with custody or control" of the tapes in question. They filed one copy with the district court clerk. The other was hand delivered to the White House by Cox team member Philip Lacovara and his U.S. marshal escort.

Back at the K Street office, Cox and his staff were deeply worried. Would the president even accept the subpoena? Would Lacovara be turned away at the White House gate? At the time, these seemed like real possibilities. But all ultimately went smoothly. White House counsel Fred Buzhardt accepted service of the subpoena "on behalf of the President" at 6:20 p.m. on July 23.[34]

There was a method behind this strategy. The president and his lawyers accepted the subpoena because they thought they would win in court. On July 25, Nixon notified Judge Sirica by letter that he would not be handing over the tapes. The president, he wrote, is "not subject to compulsory process from the courts."

At this point, Cox had three options. He could give up. He could seek to have the president held in contempt of court. Or he could seek an "order to show cause," basically a formal judicial demand for an explanation. In this case, such an order would require Nixon to explain why he should be permitted to defy the subpoena. Giving up was never seriously considered. Seeking to hold the president in contempt would represent a major escalation into even more uncharted legal territory. It might even provoke a full-blown constitutional crisis. It might also backfire. Certainly, no court would be eager to hold the president in contempt, with the steep fines and threat of imprisonment that typically entails. Seeking an order to show cause seemed much the more prudent course.[35]

Judge Sirica could have issued the order on his own authority. Instead, he took the unusual step of asking the grand jury to make the request. Even more unusually, he asked them to do so in public. Cox had been allowed to poll the jurors ahead of time, so he knew that they would vote unanimously in favor. But he was still nervous. The jury comprised nineteen ordinary citizens. Cox and Sirica were asking them to declare in a crowded, public courtroom, "Yes, okay. We want you to subpoena the President of the United States." Cox recalled, "it was a marvelously symbolic scene. There were the people of the United States calling on the highest official in the United States to do his share to contribute to the administration of justice." As expected, the vote was unanimous, and Judge Sirica ordered the president to show cause or comply with the subpoena.[36]

The president stuck to his guns and filed a brief outlining his legal defense. Oral argument was scheduled for August 22. Cox would argue the case himself. He may not have been an experienced trial lawyer, but the great constitutional questions in the subpoena fight were his bread and butter. He had argued dozens of such cases before the United States Supreme Court as solicitor general.

Charles Alan Wright would argue for the president. Fifteen years younger than Cox, Wright was similarly tall and straight-backed and shared an equally sterling educational pedigree. Like Cox, Wright was an eminent professor of constitutional law. In fact, his well-known treatise *Federal Practice and Procedure* gave him a plausible claim to preeminence in the field. The two men even bore a slight resemblance to one another. Wright, however, cut a far more commanding and self-confident figure.

Cox, by contrast, could come across as an egghead—brilliant and thoughtful but somewhat diffident and indecisive, with his head in the clouds. At 10 a.m., the two lawyers sat silently at their respective counsel tables, notes before them, facing the bench. Cox nervously spilled a glass of water. The stage was set.[37]

Wright stepped to the podium first. The special prosecutor's subpoena, he began, was without precedent "in the 184 years of this republic." And for good reason. There were four hundred district judges in the United States. If any one of them could pry into the president's most confidential papers at any time, the executive branch would cease to function. This case, Wright emphasized, was not just about Nixon. It was about all future presidents. In closing, Wright sounded a chilling note. One tape sought by the special prosecutor, he said, contained national security matters "so highly sensitive" that Nixon did not "feel free even to hint to me what the nature of it is."[38] Forcing the president to turn over the tapes would be nothing short of dangerous to the country.

Cox rose from his blue leather chair and strode to the podium. This was a "grave and dramatic case," he acknowledged. Even so, he urged Judge Sirica not to be swayed by the "false mystique" of executive privilege. Judges, Cox said, should "apply the same law to cases great and small." Wright's slippery slope argument was a distraction. The unprecedented character of this case showed that courts would seldom need to intrude on a president's privacy. Here, however, that need was compelling. "There is not merely accusation, but strong evidence that the integrity of the Executive offices has been corrupted."

Cox closed by invoking the story of King James I. In a dispute with the great English judge Lord Coke, James insisted that he could take any case away from the courts and decide it as he pleased. When Coke told him that this was contrary to the laws of England, James responded bitterly. If that were the case, he said, then "I am to be under the law, and that is treason to aver!" In a famous retort, Lord Coke replied that even the king was "under God and law." If this were true of Kings, Cox concluded, surely it was also true of presidents.[39]

The rest is history. On August 30, Sirica ordered the president to turn over the tapes. The White House defiantly declared that the president would not comply with the order, simultaneously announcing its intent to appeal. On September 12, Cox and Wright gave an encore performance of their arguments before the United States Court of Appeals. Two days later, the court issued a highly unusual order, directing the parties to work out their differences by September 20. If they could not, the court would do it for them. Both Cox's team and the president's lawyers worked diligently on a compromise, but the two sides never approached an agreement. Jointly, they advised the court that their "sincere efforts were not fruitful." Charles Wright penned a final brief on Nixon's behalf. "To tear down the office of the American presidency," it warned, "is too high a price to pay even for Watergate."

As September slid into October, the president's public approval sank to historic lows. On October 6, the Egyptian army crossed the Suez Canal in force. On October 10, Nixon's vice president, Spiro Agnew, resigned and pled no contest to one count of federal tax evasion. In exchange, prosecutors agreed to drop several other more serious corruption charges against Agnew unrelated to Watergate. On October 12, the Court of Appeals ruled in the subpoena case. It was an all-out victory for the special prosecutor. The president, the court held, "is not above the law's commands. Sovereignty remains at all times with the people, and they do no forfeit the right through elections to have the law construed against and applied to every citizen."

The clock was ticking. The president now had just days to decide whether to petition the Supreme Court for review. Most observers assumed the case would end up before the justices, but both sides had much to lose by going that route. For Cox, there was the risk of losing his Court of Appeals victory and walking away with nothing. There was also the risk of boxing the president into a corner and forcing a constitutional crisis. For Nixon, there was the risk of suffering a final, decisive defeat and losing all leverage over Cox.

With these risks in mind, compromise negotiations resumed. They mostly focused on review of the tapes by some trusted third party who could excise sensitive national security information and other privileged matter. But the president was adamantly opposed to turning over the tapes or even verbatim transcripts. At most, he would consider producing summaries, approved for accuracy by his aging, hard-of-hearing Senate ally John Stennis. Nixon also demanded unequivocally that Cox agree not to pursue any additional subpoenas. These were terribly one-sided terms, but Cox was sufficiently nervous about the alternative that he came perilously close to accepting. In the end, he could not bring himself to do it. The final White House proposal was not a compromise. It was an ultimatum.[40]

At 8:18 p.m. on October 19, Nixon press secretary Ron Ziegler announced that the White House was imposing its "compromise" solution unilaterally. The president would not comply with the Court of Appeals order. Instead, he had ordered the special prosecutor to desist from any further efforts to obtain the White House tapes. Cox heard the news over the phone from his chief press officer, James Doyle. He promptly scheduled a press conference for the next day. Twenty-four hours later, he was out of a job.[41]

The Final Act

Nixon hoped that Cox's firing would end the looming threat that Watergate posed to his administration. Instead, it did the opposite. Press coverage was universally hostile, much of it warning of creeping authoritarianism. Outraged letters and telegrams flooded the White House and congressional offices. Republicans in Congress distanced themselves from Nixon in droves. Cox himself issued a brief public statement, eloquent in its sobriety and restraint: "whether we shall continue to be a Government of laws and not of men is now for Congress and ultimately the American people."[42]

Cox's statement proved not just eloquent but prescient. A week after Nixon fired Cox, public pressure forced the President to appoint a new special prosecutor with even greater independence than Cox had enjoyed. Similar White House guarantees had not saved Cox. But after his dismissal, it was clear that any further breach would trigger Nixon's impeachment. The new special prosecutor, a brash Texan named Leon Jaworski, pursued his investigation vigorously and mostly free from presidential interference. That investigation culminated in a dramatic Supreme Court victory for the special prosecutor. The Court's decision forced the president to release dozens of severely incriminating tapes, far more than Cox had demanded. Days later, Nixon resigned rather than face impeachment.[43]

On the surface, this outcome seems distinctly improbable. President Nixon actually allowed himself to be forced from office by a special prosecutor he had the power to fire at any time. He did not go down willingly. He fought tooth and nail, viciously and without scruple, as he had done for his entire political career. So what can explain this result?[44]

The obvious answer is intense and sustained political pressure, which was made possible by the special prosecutor's high public visibility. Never has the power of special prosecutors—or the dependence of that power on the vigilance of the American people— been clearer. This outcome was not inevitable. If Nixon had not committed the extraordinary blunder of taping his Oval Office conversations, events might have played out very differently. Both the tapes and the special prosecutor were crucial to the public's ability to hold the president accountable. But as events actually un-folded, the system worked. The rule of law prevailed. For nearly fifty years, the Saturday Night Massacre has served as a cautionary tale for presidents. The moral of that tale is clear: not even the president is above the law, and any president who tries to flout this principle—in particular, by firing a special prosecutor—does so at his own peril.[45]

4

The World Watergate Made

Watergate lit a spark under official Washington like nothing before or since. Political pressure may have saved the rule of law once, but there was no guarantee it would do so again. If the president could fire a special prosecutor at will, or refuse to appoint one in the first place, could the constitutional order really be safe? What was to protect the United States from another Richard Nixon? To most of the generation that lived through Watergate, the answer seemed to be all too little.

In the aftermath of Nixon's resignation, public confidence in politicians and government institutions cratered. In 1958, only 25 percent of Americans believed the government could not generally be trusted to do what is right. By 1980, that number had risen to 76 percent. This was clearly not all about Watergate. But between 1972 and 1976 alone, mistrust in government rose from 46 to 68 percent.

Members of Congress were growing increasingly worried. Just days after the Saturday Night Massacre, Senator Birch Bayh sternly warned his colleagues on the Senate floor: "our system of government is facing a crisis of unprecedented proportions." Even cautious moderates like Senator John Glenn of Ohio, the former astronaut and Air Force pilot, thought something had to be done and called on Congress "to make every effort to restore public confidence in our institutions of government."[1]

Between 1974 and 1978, a flurry of reform measures were proposed and debated, with no single approach attracting majority support. The most ambitious proposal was to establish a permanent and fully independent special prosecutor, but opponents raised constitutional objections. Such an arrangement, they argued, would conflict with the president's power to "take care the laws be faithfully executed." Others worried that the proposal was overkill, like killing a fly with a sledgehammer. A small minority suggested that no reform was necessary because Watergate had proved that the existing system worked.[2]

By 1977, many members of Congress were getting desperate. Three years had passed since Nixon's resignation, and they had still failed to pass any meaningful reform legislation. Meanwhile, Jimmy Carter had won the presidency on the simple slogan "I'll never lie to you." This could only have sounded noble if voters assumed that most politicians *would* lie to them. "Read the papers, talk to the people," urged Florida senator Lawton Chiles. "More and more, they speak less and less of a few rotten apples. Now they look with skepticism at the entire barrel."[3]

Finally, in 1978, Congress converged on a package of reforms that became known as the Ethics in Government Act. The Senate passed the Act on October 7. The House followed suit on October 12, almost exactly five years after the Saturday Night Massacre. The law's most important provision created a new type of special prosecutor, called the independent counsel. Like ordinary special prosecutors, independent counsels would investigate and prosecute a single case or collection of related cases. But as their name implied, they were intended to operate with significantly greater independence from the president. The overriding goal was to make it more difficult for presidents to resist the appointment of special prosecutors or interfere with their investigations.

To that end, the Act created an intricate formal process for triggering the appointment of an independent counsel. Previously, this decision had been entirely within the president's discretion. Under the new law, that discretion was tightly regulated. If the Justice Department received credible allegations of criminal activity by senior executive officials, the attorney general was required to conduct a formal inquiry. If this inquiry demonstrated that the allegations were baseless, that was the end of the matter. But if it did not, the attorney general was required to refer to the matter to a special panel of federal judges. That panel would then select an independent counsel and define the limits of his or her jurisdiction. No longer would the president or his hand-picked attorney general have any role in selecting special prosecutors.

The president could still fire the independent counsel, acting through the attorney general. But this power could be exercised only for "good cause"—a legal term of art that is considerably more exacting than it sounds. Furthermore, the independent counsel was entitled to seek judicial review of the attorney general's judgment that this standard had been met. In this way, the courts would check the president's ability to fire the independent counsel for purely political reasons. The end result was a far more powerful and politically independent special prosecutor than had ever before existed in the United States. The new system accomplished its main goal of preventing another Saturday Night Massacre. But the cure was arguably worse than the disease.[4]

Best-Laid Plans

Many other countries have similarly structured independent prosecutorsand regard them as integral to the rule of law. But the independent counsel created by the Ethics in Government Act proved problematic and controversial from the outset. For one thing, the Act's trigger mechanism seemed too sensitive. It required the attorney general to seek the appointment of an independent counsel in circumstances where no private citizen would be prosecuted. For example, two high-level advisors of President Jimmy Carter were allegedly seen snorting cocaine at the notoriously louche nightclub Studio 54. No private citizen would be prosecuted for such activity. But the Ethics in Government Act did not permit the attorney general to exercise similar lenience toward high executive officials.[5]

The Act's trigger mechanism could also be manipulated by the attorney general, whose decision whether to seek appointment of an independent counsel was final and unreviewable. Ronald Reagan's attorney general Edwin Meese, a tough and irascible Republican partisan, raised such manipulation to an art form. Several times, Meese refused to seek appointment of an independent counsel because there was no clear evidence that a suspect had acted with criminal intent. Other times, Meese found allegations credible but insufficiently specific. His artful evasions led Congress to close several loopholes in the Act that he had exploited. But for constitutional reasons, the final decision whether to seek appointment of an independent counsel remained with the attorney general. This decision had to be explained to Congress, but it could not be challenged in court.[6]

There was also a far bigger and more basic problem with the Act. Presidents and their political allies lacked confidence in special prosecutors appointed by statutory edict, selected by unelected judges, and protected against dismissal by judicial review. To many Democrats, this initially seemed like a feature, rather than a bug, of the Act. During the Reagan administration, partisan Republicans railed against a series of independent counsel investigations that

Democrats thought vitally necessary. Without the tenure protec-
tions of the Ethics in Government Act, they reasoned, Ronald
Reagan might have repeated the Saturday Night Massacre. That
would have stopped independent counsel Lawrence Walsh's important investigation of the Iran-Contra affair in its tracks.

By contrast, Republicans saw Walsh as the prototypical runaway
prosecutor. In their view, his drawn-out, seven-year investigation
was an outrageous attempt to criminalize a good-faith constitutional dispute between the president and Congress. Eventually,
however, the shoe was bound to wind up on the other foot. And so
it did in 1994, with independent counsel Kenneth Starr's investigation of President Bill Clinton.[7]

That investigation easily might never have happened. The
Ethics in Government Act—the independent counsel statute, for
short— was written to require renewal every five years. On the eve
of the 1992 presidential election, Congress had allowed it to lapse.
Outgoing president George H. W. Bush hated the law, largely due
to his own experience being investigated during the Iran-Contra
affair. When Clinton won the election, Bush advised him to let it
die, but most Democrats still believed in the independent counsel.
In June 1994, Congress voted to revive it.

On the last day of that month, President Clinton signed the
bill enthusiastically, calling it "a foundation stone for trust between
the Government and our citizens." In words that would soon look
deeply ironic, he dismissed claims that the independent counsel
was "a tool of partisan attack" and a "waste of taxpayer funds." To
the contrary, Clinton said, the independent counsel "has been in the
past and is today a force for Government integrity and public confidence. This new statute enables the great work of Government to
go forward with the trust of its citizens assured."[8]

A month later, Clinton's attorney general, Janet Reno, concluded that there were "reasonable grounds" under the Act to

further investigate Bill and Hillary Clinton. The basis for this conclusion was a failed Arkansas land deal known as "Whitewater." This matter was already being investigated by Robert Fiske, a widely respected special prosecutor whom Reno had appointed before the renewal of the independent counsel statute. But out of an abundance of caution, Reno referred the matter to the Special Division of the Court of Appeals (the special panel of judges designated by the statute to oversee independent counsel investigations). Since Fiske had been appointed by the Clinton administration, the judges determined that it would be inappropriate to reappoint him. Instead, in a decision that would change history and doom the independent counsel statute to infamy, they selected former federal judge and solicitor general Kenneth Starr.[9]

Whitewater Estates

In the summer of 1978, Affirmed became the second horse in two years to win thoroughbred racing's Triple Crown. The movie musical *Grease*, starring John Travolta and Olivia Newton John, gave teenage viewers chills. And two young couples met for dinner at the Black-Eyed Pea, a down-home restaurant in Little Rock, Arkansas. At the time, the dinner did not seem especially noteworthy to either couple. Bill Clinton and Hillary Rodham frequently shared meals with Jim and Susan McDougal, and this one seemed no different from any of the others.

Bill Clinton and Jim McDougal had met a decade earlier when both worked for Senator William Fulbright. An offbeat and magnetic personality, McDougal impressed Clinton with his wit, and Clinton had charmed McDougal in return. Both seemed to have bright futures ahead of them. By 1978, McDougal had shifted his infectious enthusiasm from politics to real estate. A born huckster, he was always making grandiose predictions about his latest scheme. This night was no different, except that he invited Bill and Hillary to get in on the ground floor of a "sure thing." The picturesque Ozark Mountains north of Little Rock were a vacation paradise waiting to happen. Jim had a plan that would put them on the map. He called it "Whitewater Estates." Susan had come up with the name.

"You'll want to go in with us on this," Jim said lustily.

The terms were generous. McDougal would lend Bill and Hillary their portion of the down payment. They would also receive a lot for themselves, overlooking the scenic White River. It was the perfect spot to build a vacation home. The proceeds from the development could also serve as a "nest egg." This was no small enticement for a couple who expected to support themselves for some time on the modest salary of an Arkansas public official.

Besides friendship, McDougal's generosity probably had something to do with Bill Clinton being heavily favored in that year's race for governor. At just thirty-two, Clinton would be the youngest chief executive in Arkansas history. The chance to rub shoulders with the state's first family could be a significant draw for the development's prospective investors. In any case, after a remarkably casual twenty-minute conversation, the two couples shook hands across the red and white checked tablecloth to seal the deal. With the formal signing of papers on August 2, 1978, Bill Clinton and Hillary Rodham became part owners of Whitewater Estates.[10]

Their timing could hardly have been worse. As the economy sank into recession in the early 1980s, interest rates shot through the roof. No one was buying first homes, much less vacation properties. Meanwhile, Jim McDougal had purchased a small bank known as Madison Guaranty Savings and Loan. To shore up the debt-financed Whitewater development and to hide its sagging fortunes from his investors, he shifted assets from Madison

Guaranty. As the economy got worse, his shell games grew ever more elaborate. As Susan McDougal later recalled, "if one thing wouldn't work to fix something, he'd do seven. And they'd all be convoluted and interrelated, but none of them would work."[11]

Over the next several years, Jim McDougal would preside over an expanding but increasingly fraudulent financial business empire. His basic strategy was to use the federally insured assets of Madison Guaranty as a piggy bank. This enabled him to finance a staggering array of ill-advised real estate projects, ranging from a Little Rock subdivision to an island resort in Maine. During this period, McDougal's mental and physical health steadily deteriorated, as did his marriage to Susan. They separated in 1985, but their financial affairs remained deeply entangled.

The next year, federal regulators notified the McDougals that Madison Guaranty would be shuttered for insolvency. Shortly afterward, Jim was hospitalized for a stroke and diagnosed with bipolar disorder. In 1989, he became one of hundreds of savings and loan operators charged with defrauding the federal government. But the old magic was not entirely gone. After a mesmeric performance on the witness stand, McDougal was acquitted of all charges.[12]

Had Bill Clinton not run for president in 1992, that probably would have concluded the matter. But he did run, and politics is a dirty business, and Clinton had made his share of enemies during his twelve years as governor of Arkansas. Two of those enemies were Sheffield Nelson, chairman of the state Republican Party, and Larry Nichols, an aggrieved former state employee. A third was Jim McDougal, who felt badly slighted by Clinton's efforts to distance himself when McDougal was facing federal charges. When Nelson and Nichols came looking for stories that might damage Clinton in the national press, McDougal was only too happy to chat. As he later explained, "the Whitewater case unfolded because I wanted

Bill Clinton to feel my pain." In early March 1992, Nelson and Nichols finally got a serious journalist to bite.[13]

Jeff Gerth of the *New York Times* met Jim McDougal at a cheap buffet restaurant in the tiny town of Arkadelphia, Arkansas. They talked for several hours. On the strength of this conversation, Gerth filed a story that ran on the front page of the March 8 edition. Its prominent placement belied the story's entirely unsensational content. "Clinton Joined S & L Operator in Ozark Real-Estate Venture," ran the appropriately bland headline.

McDougal plainly nursed a grudge against the Clintons, and Sheffield Nelson had eagerly pumped him for any information that might damage Bill Clinton's candidacy. But McDougal had apparently said nothing to Gerth that implicated the Clintons in any wrongdoing. He seemed glad just to be part of the action again. Gerth's story simply and straightforwardly reported that the Clintons had partnered in a land development venture with the operator of a failed savings and loan. There was, perhaps, a faint whiff of impropriety about the story but no concrete allegation of illegal or unethical conduct by either of the Clintons.[14]

The campaign's public response was clumsy and disproportionate. But for the remainder of 1992, the whole affair never rose above a low-level nuisance. After Clinton's surprise victory over President George H. W. Bush, the Clintons assumed it was old news. To ensure that remained the case, they dispatched their friend and lawyer Vince Foster to extricate them from Whitewater once and for all. In an agreement Foster drew up, the Clintons sold their remaining interest in Whitewater to Jim McDougal for $1,000. The Clintons themselves nominally loaned this sum to McDougal, but they never expected to be repaid, and no money changed hands. The Clintons were finally free of the albatross they had been dragging around for over a decade. Or so Foster thought when he scrawled "closed for good" across the Whitewater file on December 30, 1992.[15]

A Scandal Rekindled

By the next summer, the grave, soft-spoken Foster would be dead of a self-inflicted gunshot wound in Fort Marcy Park, just off the George Washington Parkway. He was forty-seven. Overwhelmed by the pressures of his new job as deputy White House counsel, Foster had been depressed and withdrawn for months. Ultimately, he broke under the strain. Among the items in his portfolio at the time was Whitewater, which had continued to receive occasional press coverage. Amid the frenzied speculation and overheated conspiracy theories that followed Foster's death, Whitewater generated white-hot new interest. Had Foster been hiding a terrible secret that drove him to suicide? Had he actually been murdered by the Clintons or their agents to ensure his silence? Outlandish as these questions may sound, they received more than respectful attention in much of the conservative press. They also revived a burning interest in Whitewater just when the ember of scandal seemed nearly to have gone out. As author James Stewart put it, Foster's suicide "brought it all back. I mean, if Vince Foster hadn't killed himself, it would have all gone away."[16]

Into this maelstrom walked an Arkansas small businessman named David Hale. A former national president of the Jaycees, the rumpled and oleaginous Hale was facing federal charges in Arkansas for conspiring to defraud the federal Small Business Administration. According to federal prosecutors, he had misused funds he was supposed to have lent to minority- and women-owned businesses. One of Hale's fraudulent schemes involved James and Susan McDougal, as prosecutors had long known. But Hale now added a new wrinkle to the story. Bill Clinton, he said, had pressured him to lend money to Susan McDougal under false pretenses, in order to prop up the failing Whitewater development.

In 1986, when his rickety financial empire was teetering on the verge of collapse, Jim McDougal came to Hale with a proposal. Hale had federal money to loan to women. Susan McDougal was a woman. Why didn't Hale loan $300,000 to her marketing firm? Jim could then use the money to shore up his other ventures, including Whitewater. The first several times Hale told this story, he never mentioned Bill Clinton. Then the former Arkansas governor was elected president. Hale hoped that this would change everything. In exchange for implicating the president, Hale hoped to receive leniency, either from the U.S. attorney prosecuting him or, better yet, a special prosecutor appointed specifically to investigate Bill Clinton. He struck out with the U.S. attorney. That meant he would have to get a special prosecutor appointed.[17]

Throughout the fall of 1993, Hale peddled his story to the *Washington Post*, the *Los Angeles Times*, and the *New York Times*. He was shepherded from one reporter to the next by a man named Cliff Jackson, another old Clinton enemy from Arkansas. An attorney and former Oxford classmate of Clinton, Jackson was the principal mover behind another scandal known as "Troopergate." Several former state troopers alleged that Clinton had used them to procure women during his tenure as governor. Jackson tried to sell their story through the national media, without notable success.

Having failed once himself, Jackson put Hale in touch with his media contacts. In the fall of 1994, most major media organizations remained cautious about the Whitewater story. But the press coverage from this period reads in retrospect like a gathering storm. The storm clouds finally burst in December. That is when the press first reported that White House counsel Bernie Nussbaum had removed Whitewater-related documents from Vince Foster's office following his suicide. The ostensible motive for this action was that the documents contained privileged attorney-client communications. But even if that were correct, the retrieval was handled haphazardly, at best. From this point forward, new calls to appoint a special prosecutor became an almost daily occurrence.[18]

The crisis point for the administration arrived on January 11. Clinton was touring central Europe to discuss the expansion of NATO, but the only thing reporters wanted to discuss at his press appearances was Whitewater. Back at his hotel in Prague that night, the President convened a conference call with his closest advisors in Washington. Should he relent and request that the attorney general appoint a special prosecutor? The Whitewater story was all anyone could talk about. He could not conduct business this way.[19]

His advisors were split. Hillary Clinton and Bernie Nussbaum counseled strongly against it. Nussbaum's warning was especially prescient. "The frustration of finding nothing in Whitewater will make them investigate every one of your friends," he said. "If we allow this, it will be a knife in the heart of this presidency. Nothing happened with Whitewater. But the investigation will range all over." Policy advisor George Stephanopoulos interjected that they should just appoint a special prosecutor and be done with it. "This will be over in six months," he predicted. Nussbaum vehemently disagreed, spelling out in lurid detail the kind of investigation he would carry out if he were appointed special prosecutor. It was past 2 a.m. in Prague. Finally, the exhausted president weighed in. "You're telling me I can't do it, Bernie, but I'm being killed!" The next morning Clinton formally requested that Janet Reno appoint a special prosecutor.[20]

A Starr Is Born

Reno tapped deputy attorney general Philip Heymann, a veteran of the Watergate task force, to conduct the search. On his recommendation, she appointed Robert Fiske, a sixty-three-year-old former U.S. attorney and a Republican. Besides extensive prosecutorial experience, the compact, no-nonsense Fiske had a well-earned reputation for political independence. In Reno's and Heymann's view, this made him an ideal choice. Since Fiske had voted for George Bush over Bill Clinton, they could not be accused of rigging the investigation in Clinton's favor. But neither did they need to fear a partisan witch hunt. Fiske had been on the job for just over six months when the Special Division of the Court of Appeals replaced him with Kenneth Starr.[21]

Born in 1946, the same year as Bill Clinton, Ken Starr spent his formative years in San Antonio, Texas, where his father worked as a part-time minister. Serious and devout, Starr began his college education at Harding, a conservative Church of Christ school in tiny Searcy, Arkansas. In many ways, this was an ideal environment for him, but he also hungered for new challenges and a taste of the wider world. After two years, he transferred to George Washington University. From there, he moved on to Duke Law School.

Starr rose to the highest echelons of the American legal profession with extraordinary speed. First, he earned a coveted clerkship on the U.S. Supreme Court for Chief Justice Warren Burger. That distinction won him an important post in the Justice Department under William French Smith, Ronald Reagan's first attorney general. Finally, on Smith's and Burger's recommendations, Reagan appointed Starr to the United States Court of Appeals for the District of Columbia in 1983. At just thirty-seven years old, Starr was—and remains—the youngest person ever to serve on this court, the second most important in the country.[22]

After a brief five years on the bench, Starr was persuaded to resign in order to serve as solicitor general under Ronald Reagan's successor, George H. W. Bush. He gave up his life-tenured position reluctantly, apparently expecting that he would be considered for a Supreme Court appointment the next time a vacancy arose. It was not to be. After stepping down as solicitor general in January 1993, Starr joined the high-powered law firm Kirkland & Ellis. He had been in private practice just over a year when he accepted the appointment as independent counsel for Whitewater.

Balding and bespectacled, with cherubic features and a highly developed sense of rectitude, Starr brought obvious strengths to the job. He was universally recognized as a lawyer of high integrity and ability. Politically, he had a reputation as a moderate and mild-mannered conservative with a conciliatory temperament. But Starr was also unquestionably a more partisan figure than Robert Fiske. He moved in the same social and professional circles as many committed movement conservatives.

Starr was also notably lacking in prosecutorial experience—or, for that matter, any substantial trial experience. Like Archibald Cox, Starr had spent virtually all of his career in the rarefied, almost academic world of appellate litigation, especially at the Supreme Court. When Janet Reno's deputy Philip Heymann briefly considered Starr before appointing Fiske, he saw this as a dangerous combination. Without meaningful prosecutorial experience, Starr would be forced to rely heavily on his subordinates, and those subordinates were likely "to be Republican fanatics, not balanced mainline prosecutors." Heymann had been unwilling to take this risk.[23]

The Court of Appeals judges who selected Starr evidently did not share this concern. In a unanimous order, dated August 5, 1994, they appointed him independent counsel. The same order authorized Starr to investigate whether "any individuals or entities" had committed a federal crime "relating in any way" to the Whitewater land development, Jim McDougal's savings and loan, or David Hale's fraudulent lending operation. Two of the three judges on the panel, David Sentelle and Joseph

Sneed, were hardline conservatives. It later emerged that the third judge and sole Democrat on the panel, John D. Butzner, had strongly opposed the selection of Starr. As Butzner saw it, that selection violated the court's long-standing policy against appointing Washington lawyers with strong ties to either political party. When Butzner realized that he would not persuade his colleagues, he switched his vote to protect the reputation of the court.[24]

"You Can't Rectify All the Wrongs in the World"

For the next five years, Starr presided over an ever-expanding investigation of the president, first lady Hillary Clinton, and their former Arkansas associates. After reaching a generous deal with David Hale, Starr and his team successfully prosecuted Jim and Susan McDougal for defrauding the Small Business Administration of $300,000. Jim McDougal was also convicted of more than a dozen other counts related to Madison Guaranty. At the same trial, Bill Clinton's successor as governor, Jim Guy Tucker, was convicted of mail fraud in connection with Madison Guaranty.[25] Separately, Starr's team successfully prosecuted former associate attorney general Webster Hubbell for billing fraud at Hillary Clinton's Arkansas law firm. Most of the fraud was against the firm, making Hillary one of its victims.

Following his conviction, James McDougal cooperated with Starr's team, hoping to obtain a reduced sentence. After years of denials, he corroborated Hale's story that Clinton had pressured Hale to make the fraudulent $300,000 loan to Susan McDougal. But by this point, McDougal was a very sick and mentally unstable individual. He had been convicted of multiple felonies and possessed strong incentives to lie to cut down his own prison time. His testimony was not nearly enough—even combined with Hale's testimony, given under similar circumstances—to bring criminal charges against the president.

Still, Starr and his team remained convinced that Susan McDougal, Webster Hubbell, and Jim Guy Tucker were holding back evidence that would convict the Clintons. To make these recalcitrant witnesses talk, Starr's prosecutors kept up a relentless pressure on all three. They had Susan McDougal jailed for contempt of court and brought several additional charges against Hubbell and Tucker, unrelated to Whitewater or Madison Guaranty. None of the three would ever implicate Bill or Hillary Clinton in any wrongdoing.[26]

Meanwhile, Starr's investigation repeatedly morphed in other directions. Ultimately, it encompassed the death of Vince Foster, which Robert Fiske had already thoroughly investigated; the Clintons' firing of White House Travel Office employees, allegedly to install Clinton cronies in their place; and Hillary Clinton's alleged mishandling of secret FBI files. By late 1997, Starr and his office seemed to have fallen victim to an obsessive mindset. To paraphrase Italo Calvino, they resembled a writer "for whom the least thing is seen as the center of a network of relationships that the writer cannot restrain himself from following, multiplying the details, so that his descriptions and digressions become infinite. Whatever the starting point, the matter in hand spreads out and out, encompassing ever vaster horizons, and if it were permitted to go further and further in every direction, it would end by embracing the entire universe."[27]

This, former independent counsel Jacob Stein warned, was not how a responsible special prosecutor should behave. "I think someone with the power the office confers should recognize that you cannot rectify all of the wrongs in the world," he told a group of assembled judges in 1997. "You can't pursue all the leads that come to you; and you've got to have the courage to close the investigation in spite of the fact that just when you are ready to close it, you get a letter from somebody who says he has got the goods on your man—he's got the goods and he will produce a woman in your office 10:30 tomorrow morning to blow this investigation wide open." With all the other strands of their investigation petering out or wrapping up, this was precisely the position Starr and his team found themselves in on January 12, 1998.[28]

A Bridge Too Far

"It's me," croaked a raspy female voice on the other end of the line. It was nearly 10 p.m., and Jackie Bennett was working late, but these two words were enough to make his face light up. A former federal prosecutor from Indiana with the build of an offensive lineman, Bennett was Ken Starr's principal deputy in Washington, D.C. He had been waiting for this call all day. "This is her!" he mouthed exaggeratedly, urgently beckoning the other lawyers and FBI agents into his office. No one had to ask whom he meant.[29]

The previous weekend, a newer member of Starr's team had taken the train to Philadelphia to spend an evening with two old law school classmates. Just shy of forty, Paul Rosenzweig had a somewhat quirky personality and a partiality for bow ties. He had no idea what awaited him when he walked into the opulent lobby of Berger & Montague, where his friend Jerome Marcus worked as an attorney. The two men greeted each other warmly and settled into a couple of comfortable lounge chairs for a predinner chat.

Marcus could barely contain his excitement. For more than a year, he had been secretly helping with a sexual harassment lawsuit that a former Arkansas employee named Paula Jones had brought against President Clinton. Through his connection with the case, Marcus had recently learned something stunning. Bill Clinton had been carrying on a sexual relationship with a young woman at the

White House. Both were lying or planning to lie about it in the Jones case, which was then pending in a federal district court in Arkansas. In exchange for keeping quiet, the president's girlfriend would receive help finding a job from the president's all-purpose fixer, Vernon Jordan. These were not just secondhand rumors. There was a witness with tapes that proved everything.[30]

Somewhat skeptical but also intrigued, Rosenzweig dutifully carried the message back to his superiors in Washington. In retrospect, he would reflect, his conversation with Marcus was "probably the most significant moment of my life." He would also feel a bit used—like his friend had "taken advantage of our relationship." At the time, however, Rosenzweig had more pressing concerns. One loomed particularly large: Were these explosive allegations even within the independent counsel's jurisdiction?[31]

At first, as the team members discussed it, the answer seemed obviously to be no. The allegations simply had no connection with Whitewater or the other matters they had been authorized to investigate over the years. But as they mulled it over, one slight point of connection suggested itself. While investigating Webster Hubbell, Starr's lawyers came to believe that Vernon Jordan had arranged for hush money to keep Hubbell quiet about the Clintons. A assignment job to keep Clinton's girlfriend quiet seemed eerily similar. Both amounted to possible obstruction of justice orchestrated by the same close associate of the president. Starr was out of town, so Jackie Bennett made the call. They would pursue the lead, but the witness had to come to them directly.[32]

The witness was Linda Tripp, a disgruntled former White House employee who now worked at the Department of Defense alongside a young woman named Monica Lewinsky. Tense, chatty, paranoid, and shrewd, Tripp nursed a deep and somewhat mysterious sense of grievance against the Clintons. For several months, she had actively cultivated a maternal friendship with the bubbly, emotional, and much younger Lewinsky. Eventually and rather coyly, Lewinsky let on that she had been romantically involved with someone high up at the White House during her previous job. Finally, she confessed that her love interest was the president. Sensing an opportunity, Tripp drew Lewinsky out about the relationship in long telephone conversations that she secretly—and illegally—taped. The recordings revealed lurid details of Lewinsky's sexual assignations with the president. They also captured Lewinsky's anxious reaction when she received a subpoena to testify in the Paula Jones case and her desperate strategies for concealing her relationship with the president.[33]

In a nervous, disjointed narrative, Tripp related this improbable story to Jackie Bennett over the phone. She also mentioned that she had a lunch date with Lewinsky the next day and would be willing to wear a wire. Bennett had heard enough. "We're coming out," he said. That night, Bennett, two other prosecutors, and an FBI agent drove to Tripp's house in suburban Columbia, Maryland. Bluegrass music blared from the stereo of their white minivan for much of the way. They interviewed Tripp for several hours. Finding her allegations credible, they arranged for her to wear a state-of-the-art digital recording device to her lunch with Lewinsky the next day. The game was afoot.[34]

Death Comes for the Independent Counsel

The rest is history. The broad outlines of Tripp's account checked out, but many of the crucial details were more ambiguous than she had presented them. About some, she was simply mistaken, in part because Lewinsky had lost trust in her and deliberately withheld or misrepresented important facts. It was true that Lewinsky had a sexual relationship with the president, which mostly involved meeting him secretly at the White House for oral sex. Clinton falsely denied having any such relationship in his deposition in the Paula Jones lawsuit, when the questions caught him by surprise. (Linda Tripp had been in touch with Jones's lawyers before she contacted the independent counsel's office.) In videotaped testimony before Starr's grand jury, Clinton admitted to "inappropriate, intimate contact" with Lewinsky. But he refused to discuss the details and falsely denied that he had committed perjury in the Jones lawsuit deposition. He also shaded the truth on several other less important matters.[35]

Clinton also fairly blatantly, if not explicitly, coached his secretary, Betty Currie, to lie about his relationship with Lewinsky. At the time, however, Currie had not yet been named as a witness in any judicial proceeding. Clinton may also have asked Currie to retrieve a box of gifts he had given to Lewinsky, to prevent them from falling into the hands of Paula Jones's lawyers. But the evidence on this point is equivocal. Clinton definitely enlisted Vernon Jordan to help Monica Lewinsky find a job in New York. But at the time, he did not know that she would be called as a witness. Jordan's efforts may or may not have intensified after Lewinsky was named as a witness in the Jones case. Here, too, the evidence is ambiguous. Finally, throughout several days of testimony before federal prosecutors, the grand jury, and Congress, Monica Lewinsky consistently denied that she had ever been asked to lie or promised a job for her silence.[36]

For much of its five years of existence, Starr's investigation dominated the headlines. As year followed year, fraudulent business deals gave way to illegal campaign contributions, which gave way to indecent exposure in hotel rooms, Oval Office blow jobs, and one infamous semen-stained blue dress from The Gap. With every fresh turn of the screw, Clinton and his supporters grew more convinced that Starr's goal was "regime change" by any means necessary. Like previous administrations, Clinton and his advisors savaged Starr in the press, painting him as an ideological zealot leading a team of true believers. Later, when the Lewinsky scandal broke, they added "sex-obsessed prude" to their list of epithets for the prim and sanctimonious Starr. But Clinton, unlike previous presidents, was not free to remove the independent counsel at will—that is, for any reason at all. His hands were tied by the Ethics in Government Act, which a nearly unanimous Supreme Court had upheld as constitutional in 1988. This restriction reduced the risk of illegitimate political interference with an independent counsel's investigation, but it also eliminated any political check on an independent counsel's abuse of power or failure of judgment.[37]

The direct result was President Clinton's impeachment by the House of Representatives for perjury and obstruction of justice on December 19, 1998. A divided Senate acquitted him of these charges on February 12, 1999. Both charges stemmed from the Paula Jones case, a civil suit engineered by the enemies of a sitting president. Both concerned alleged lying and obstruction of justice about a consensual sexual relationship entirely unrelated to the sexual harassment alleged by Paula Jones. At the end of this long and sordid saga, most legal experts—and most Americans—were inclined to agree with President Clinton: an unchecked independent counsel was a cure worse than the disease. As Clinton summed it up, "after Starr came in, there was no pretext about what he and all of his supporters were doing. I felt they were Wile E. Coyote in the pack and I was the Roadrunner. And the chase was on."[38]

Like many of Clinton's pronouncements about Starr's investigation, this one is pithy and contains an element of truth. It is also self-serving, self-pitying, and unfair. In particular, the suggestion that Starr and his team were out to get the president from Day 1 is unsupported by the historical record. The truth is more nuanced. Through some combination of inexperience, unconscious ideological bias, and the nature of the independent counsel assignment,

Ken Starr lost any real sense of proportion or humility. As former independent counsel Lawrence Walsh observed, "perjury cases are difficult. Regularly appointed prosecutors generally eschew perjury prosecutions except when the perjury blocks a criminal investigation." Ordinary prosecutors are also "very wary of being drawn into private civil litigation concerning conflicting claims of sexual activity." In Walsh's view, Starr's frequent, sanctimonious invocations of "the truth" revealed "an overblown sense of his responsibility."[39]

Arkansas senator Dale Bumpers put the essential point succinctly. In a homespun closing argument at Clinton's impeachment trial, Bumpers told his Senate colleagues: "there is a total lack of proportionality, a total lack of balance in this thing. The charge and the punishment are totally out of sync." Legal analyst Benjamin Wittes offered a complementary diagnosis: "Starr's great error was in divesting himself of the discretion to behave with discretion." Just because an independent counsel *can* pursue a lead or bring a charge does not mean he *should*.[40]

Starr plainly understood this on an intellectual level. He also demonstrated the good judgment not to indict Hillary Clinton or to file an impeachment report over Whitewater. But in the Monica Lewinsky investigation, his judgment failed him. The unlimited resources at his disposal, the statutory charge to "have at" the president, combined with Starr's near total independence, produced a sort of intoxication. This was the conclusion of former Justice Department lawyer Jo Ann Harris, who formally investigated the Starr team's alleged abuses. Harris's report remains confidential, but in a post-retirement interview, she reflected: "I think everyone I talked to was absolutely persuaded, including Ken Starr, that Bill Clinton was a low-life who would lie about anything. And this happens to prosecutors—though fortunately not very often—that they would have done virtually anything to get him." This is a risk in any special prosecutor investigation, but the incentive structure created by the independent counsel statute exacerbated it considerably.[41]

Whatever the precise nature of the problem, the independent counsel statute fell into nearly universal disfavor in the aftermath of Starr's investigation. The relative approval ratings of the president and the independent counsel spoke volumes. Clinton's topped 70 percent. Starr's barely cracked 25. The support of the American people allowed Clinton to survive his ordeal, but the damage to his ability to govern was considerable. Justice Antonin Scalia's lone dissent in the 1988 Supreme Court case suddenly seemed eerily prescient. Many legal experts speculated that the independent counsel would be held unconstitutional if the issue came before the Court again.[42]

When the independent counsel statute came up for renewal in 1999, it was virtually without supporters. Attorney General Reno testified against it, and so, remarkably, did Starr. Both emphasized the importance of political oversight of special prosecutor investigations, though both also acknowledged the pitfalls. As Starr summed it up, "returning authority over these prosecutions to Attorneys General, and relying on them to appoint outside counsel when necessary, is the worst system, except for all the others."[43]

In the end, Congress allowed the Act to die a quiet and unmourned death. Two decades later, the era of the independent counsel is widely understood to illustrate an essential lesson: politics is just as important a check on special prosecutors as it is on presidents. Neither can be safely allowed to operate with impunity.

5

A New Balance

The expiration of the independent counsel statute left a void. After the Clinton impeachment ordeal, few wished to resurrect a strongly independent special prosecutor. But did anyone want to return to the wholly unregulated approach of the previous era? Was there not some middle ground? In the waning days of the Clinton administration, Attorney General Janet Reno convened a task force to answer this question.

Chaired by legal wunderkind Neal Katyal, this group of crack government lawyers rose to the challenge Reno set for them. The intricate rules they drafted had one overarching goal—to strike a balance. On the one hand, impartial and independent special prosecutors were clearly necessary to handle investigations of the president and his high-level advisors. On the other hand, special prosecutors clearly needed to be ultimately accountable to some higher authority.

The rules strike this balance by publicly committing the attorney general to appoint a special prosecutor any time credible allegations of wrongdoing require it. They also commit the attorney general not to fire special prosecutors or countermand their decisions without good reason. If the attorney general takes either of these actions, the rules require that the reasons for this decision be explained in writing to the congressional leadership of both parties.

None of these commitments is legally binding, in the traditional sense. A president can always break them, as Richard Nixon broke the commitments Elliott Richardson made to Archibald Cox. No court would, or could, intervene. But by making the commitments publicly in advance, the rules ensure that any breach will be highly visible. This gives Congress and the American people the opportunity to exact a swift and severe political price. Whether the people choose to do so is, as always, up to them.

For almost twenty years, the new rules went largely untested. Then Donald Trump was elected president.

Behind the Veil of Ignorance

Neal Katyal showed up for work at the Justice Department for the first time in January 1998. On his first day, he was supposed to meet his new boss, Eric Holder, for lunch. The savvy, mustachioed Holder was then Janet Reno's deputy attorney general, the second-highest-ranking official in the department. The bright-eyed and brilliant Katyal would be among his top lieutenants. Lunch, however, was canceled. It would be another two weeks before Katyal and Holder had a substantial conversation. Later, Katyal learned that his first day of work had also been the day that Holder first learned of the emerging Monica Lewinsky situation. Katyal did not know it then, but the Starr investigation and its aftermath would become the central focus of his time at the Justice Department.[1]

Fresh-faced, with movie-star good looks, Neal Katyal was just shy of his twenty-ninth birthday when he started work at the department. Already he had packed a startling array of accomplishments into his three decades of life. The son of Indian immigrants, Katyal demonstrated his talents for oral advocacy early. He was one of the best high school and college debaters in the country. After falling just short of a national college debate championship, he enjoyed a stellar career at Yale Law School. That career included one summer working under John Roberts, the future chief justice of the United States, at an elite Washington law firm. After graduating, Katyal advanced to highly coveted clerkships with federal Court of Appeals judge Guido Calabresi and U.S. Supreme Court justice Stephen Breyer. These jobs, which amount to one-year apprenticeships at the foot of an eminent judge, are the most prestigious credentials a budding lawyer can aspire to. At twenty-seven, Katyal parlayed them into a teaching position at Georgetown Law School, where he became one of the youngest professors in that institution's history.[2]

Law professors have two principal responsibilities. They teach classes and they write academic articles. In one of his first published articles, Katyal presciently examined the potential of the Paula Jones case to interfere with the president's constitutional duties. Before anyone had heard of Monica Lewinsky, he thought this potential was dangerously high. To eliminate this risk, Katyal argued that presidents should be immune from private lawsuits while in office. He was also an avowed skeptic of the independent counsel statute years before Ken Starr's investigation made it notorious. In Katyal's view, the power to prosecute crimes belonged exclusively to the president. The independent counsel statute had "tried to fragment this power in ways that eviscerated accountability." On the strength of these qualifications, Janet Reno tasked him with leading the Justice Department's effort to develop a more accountable special prosecutor.[3]

The timing was propitious. With Bill Clinton nearing the end of his second term, no one knew who the next president would be. Both political parties were united in their opposition to the independent counsel statute. Democrats associated the law with Ken

Starr, and Republicans associated it with the Iran-Contra debacle. As Katyal remembers it, this enabled the task force to function behind a "veil of ignorance." It was impossible to predict whose ox the new rules might gore. Both parties, therefore, could "really think through the best solution to the perennial problem of who shall guard the guardians. It was the rare time in government when it was really possible to do the right thing."[4]

That did not mean the task force's work was easy or smooth. At least since Watergate, America's best legal minds had thought long and hard about how best to investigate and prosecute the president and his top advisors. The independent counsel statute was the best solution they had come up with. The problem was intractable. A special prosecutor could not be both accountable to the president and free to operate independent of presidential interference or supervision. As Katyal would later put it, "accountability and independence are, at bottom, mutually exclusive."[5]

Yet both are desirable, at least up to a point. An insufficiently accountable special prosecutor could easily go off the rails, as Ken Starr had done. An insufficiently independent special prosecutor would always operate under a cloud of suspicion. The trick was to find an appropriate balance between these competing goods, recognizing that no solution would be perfect. To arrive at such a balance would take Katyal and his colleagues eighteen months of intense deliberation and debate, including extensive consultation with congressional staff members of both political parties.[6]

Lessons from the Past

As a starting point, the task force began with two lessons from Watergate and one from the Ken Starr investigation. Watergate showed that some investigations the Justice Department cannot credibly handle itself. The attorney general is simply too close to the president to supervise an investigation implicating the highest levels of the executive branch. The public would never trust the results. Watergate also showed the desirability of having a carefully wrought procedural framework in place ahead of time. That way, the attorney general would not be "left in the position of scrambling to set up an acceptable ad hoc alternative under the pressure of a crisis." Ken Starr's investigation showed that a fully independent special prosecutor is an unchecked force—a sort of "headless fourth branch of government," responsible to no one. Above all, the new rules could not replicate this problem.[7]

Building on these lessons, the task force drafted an elaborate set of regulations establishing a new kind of special prosecutor, which they called a "special counsel." Regulations are simply rules adopted by an executive branch agency, in this case the Justice Department. Many regulations function just like laws passed by Congress, establishing binding standards of conduct for private citizens and businesses. Think auto emissions standards or workplace safety requirements. But the regulations drafted by Katyal's task force were purely for the Justice Department's own internal use. Their concluding paragraph underlined this point with an explicit and ironclad disclaimer: "the regulations in this part are not intended to, do not, and may not be relied upon to create any rights, substantive or procedural, enforceable at law or equity, by any person or entity, in any matter, civil, criminal, or administrative." Put simply, no one could enforce the new regulations in court.[8]

That was not their purpose. Rather, the new regulations were meant to establish the kind of detailed framework that Elliott Richardson lacked at the outset of the Watergate investigation. Instead of writing on a blank slate under the pressure of events, future attorneys general would have a ready-made template from which to work. That template addressed mundane issues like staffing, budgets, and office space. But it also nudged the balance between independence and accountability sharply toward the latter. "Shoved" might be a better word.[9]

The details are boring but important. In stark contrast to the independent counsel statute, the new regulations leave the decision whether to appoint a special prosecutor entirely to the attorney general. If the answer is yes, the regulations empower the attorney general, rather than a panel of judges, to select and appoint a special counsel, subject only to a few fairly loose requirements. The one inflexible command is that special counsels be "selected from outside the federal government."[10]

Once appointed, special counsels operate "outside the day to day supervision of any official in the Department." This does not mean that they are wholly independent. The regulations empower the attorney general to seek "an explanation of any investigative step" and, in extreme cases, to override the special counsel's decisions. Unlike the independent counsel, special counsels are not required, or even permitted, to provide any report on their work to Congress. Rather, at the conclusion of the investigation, the attorney general decides whether to publish or send the special counsel's confidential final report to Congress.

Finally, the new regulations require special counsels to follow Justice Department policies, absent special permission from the attorney general. They also give the attorney general, rather than the courts, the final say on whether a special counsel should be dismissed for cause. To hammer the point home, the regulations specifically identify failure to follow departmental policy as an adequate cause for the attorney general to dismiss a special counsel.[11]

Let the Sun Shine In

The upshot was that special counsels would be on a much tighter leash than independent counsels, like Ken Starr, had been. In some ways, they would be on a tighter leash than Watergate special prosecutors Archibald Cox and Leon Jaworski. As a result, the attorney general would possess greater power to police any abuses or failures of judgment on a special counsel's part. The attorney general would also possess greater power to interfere with a special counsel's work for purely political reasons. Since the attorney general is often a party insider, who can be fired at will by the president, Katyal and his colleagues recognized that this was a major risk.

To counteract that risk, the regulations prescribed what Katyal poetically called "sunlight"—that is, transparency. By adopting the regulations, the attorney general made a standing public commitment not to interfere with or fire a special counsel without good reason. The attorney general also made a standing public commitment not to take these steps without a written explanation to Congress. In short, the attorney general—and thus the president—retains the power to crush a special counsel investigation that hits too close to home. But that power can only be exercised in broad daylight, in full view of Congress and the American people.[12]

Katyal and others have frequently described the new regulations as seeking a "more proper balance" between accountability and independence. It is easy to see what they mean. In a deeper sense, however, the regulations are all about accountability. To reduce the risk of another runaway special prosecutor, they make special counsels more accountable to the attorney general—and thus, indirectly, to the attorney general's boss, the president. To reduce the risk of improper interference with special counsel investigations, the regulations make the attorney general and the president more accountable to the American people. They do this by making the whole process as transparent as possible. If the attorney general were to break any of the commitments made in the new regulations, the press would report that breach widely.

The people could then punish the president at the polls or pressure Congress to take action.

In the summer of 2000, Attoreny General Reno announced the new regulations to broad, bipartisan acclaim. Katyal reflected on his work with satisfaction. "I felt really good about it," he recalled. "I felt like I was restoring the founders' vision of the Constitution." Katyal's Justice Department colleague James Robinson was somewhat more circumspect. A law professor and Justice Department veteran, Robinson took pride in the thoughtfulness of the task force's deliberations. On the other hand, he acknowledged that the questions addressed by the new regulations were "exceedingly difficult" and "may have no perfect solution." The proof would be in the pudding. Only by giving the regulations "a chance to work," Robinson said, would it be possible "to assess how well they fulfill their goals."[13]

When Robinson spoke these words, Donald Trump was a brash real estate impresario, famous for ostentatious displays of wealth, serial bankruptcies, and fast living. He had no political profile to speak of. Reality television, which would launch Trump to new heights of celebrity, was still in its infancy. The first episode of *The Apprentice* would not air for another three years. Anyone who predicted that President Trump would put the special counsel regulations to their first serious test would have been laughed out of the room. After November 2016, no one was laughing.

A Fateful Day at the Senate

One of the most important episodes of Donald Trump's presidency occurred on January 10, 2017, ten days before he took the oath of office. Early that morning, the elfin, white-haired senior senator from Alabama arrived at the U.S. Capitol with ten members of his family in tow. For twenty years, Jefferson Beauregard Sessions

III had called the Senate home, but this was not an ordinary day at the office. Sessions was Donald Trump's nominee for attorney general of the United States, and this was the day of his confirmation hearing. In just a few hours, he would appear before the same Senate Judiciary Committee on which he had served for many years.

As the hearing commenced, Sessions sat stiffly in the gallery of the august, marble-columned Senate chamber. His two-year-old granddaughter Hannah squirmed adorably in his lap, but the expression on the senator's face was grim, almost stricken. Although Sessions was personally friendly with many members of the committee, he could not have expected smooth sailing. Civil rights groups and other liberal activists had come out in force against his nomination. More than a thousand law professors from forty-nine states had signed a petition opposing his confirmation.[14]

No Trump cabinet nominee, with the possible exception of education secretary Betsy DeVos, had triggered such ferocious opposition. The charges of racism that had dogged Sessions much of his career would be pressed vigorously. So would charges of homophobia and complicity in voter suppression. Senators of both parties were also sure to interrogate him about his willingness to stand up to President Trump. All of this must have weighed on his mind as Sessions strode to the witness table, raised his right hand, and swore "to tell the whole truth, nothing but the truth, so help me God."[15]

The hearing did not disappoint. Sessions spent much of it indignantly defending his record on race and vowing to place the rule of law above personal loyalty to the president. Amid all this sound and fury, a late afternoon exchange with Senator Al Franken of Minnesota went virtually unnoticed. As part of a larger colloquy about Russia, the former *Saturday Night Live* comedian Franken asked Sessions a simple question. What would he do if he learned that members of the Trump campaign had communicated with the Russian government? Sessions responded that he was unaware of any such communications. He then added, somewhat gratuitously, "I did not have any communications with the Russians." A week later, in a written follow-up to questions from Vermont senator Patrick Leahy, Sessions again stated under oath that he had not "been in contact with anyone connected to any part of the Russian government about the 2016 election."[16]

The first of these statements was false. As Sessions would later admit, he had spoken with Russian ambassador Sergey Kislyak multiple times during the 2016 presidential campaign. The second, written statement was probably false and at the very least misleading. According to U.S. intelligence intercepts, Kislyak informed his superiors that he and Sessions had discussed "campaign-related matters, including policy issues important to Moscow." These misstatements led directly to the appointment of former FBI director Robert Mueller as special counsel to investigate the Trump campaign's relations with Russia.[17]

A Siberian Candidate?

Throughout the 2016 presidential campaign, Russia was an unusually salient issue. As a candidate, Donald Trump frequently expressed sympathy for Russia and admiration for Russian president Vladimir Putin. These views made Trump an extreme outlier within his own Republican Party. The more traditional Republican line, well expressed by Senator Marco Rubio, was that "Russia is governed today by a gangster." Vladimir Putin, Rubio continued, is "basically an organized crime figure who controls a government and a large territory. If you're a political adversary of Vladimir Putin, you wind up with plutonium in your drink or shot in the street." Trump, by contrast, openly basked in Putin's flattery—repeatedly noting, with evident relish, that Putin had called him a "genius." He consistently refused to criticize the Russian leader and expressed a desire for warmer relations with Russia.[18]

On July 27, 2016, Trump stood before a group of reporters in Florida, wearing a dark suit and red power tie. Asked about news reports that Russia had hacked servers at the Democratic National Committee, he blithely dismissed the possibility that the Russians were responsible. "Nobody knows who it is," he insisted in his characteristically aggressive, blustering style. Punctuating his speech with emphatic hand gestures reminiscent of an orchestra conductor, Trump continued. "I will tell you this, Russia. If you're listening, I hope you're able to find the 30,000 emails that are missing. I think you will probably be rewarded mightily by our press." The reference was to deleted emails from Hillary Clinton's private server, which had come to dominate the Republican argument against Clinton's candidacy. Democratic reactions were predictably apoplectic. "This has to be the first time that a major presidential candidate has actively encouraged a foreign power to conduct espionage against his political opponent," a Clinton campaign adviser declared. "That's not hyperbole, those are just the facts."[19]

Meanwhile, an extensive web of clandestine contacts was developing between the Trump campaign and various individuals apparently acting on behalf of the Russian government. On April 27, 2016, a naïve young American named George Papadopoulos arrived at a London hotel for a breakfast appointment. He was met by Joseph Mifsud, a shadowy Maltese professor and diplomatic hanger-on. "Cunning" and prone to "braggadocio," the beefy, gray-haired Mifsud had by this point been cultivating Papadopoulos for several weeks. His interest began when he learned that the younger man had recently been named as a foreign policy advisor to Donald Trump's presidential campaign. Boasting of high-level connections with the Russian government, Mifsud had already introduced

Papadopoulos to a woman falsely posing as Vladimir Putin's niece. Now, the professor dangled an even bigger plum. The Russians, he told Papadopoulos, had "dirt" on Hillary Clinton, consisting of thousands of stolen emails. Mifsud may also have offered Russian assistance in disseminating the messages.[20]

A few weeks later, Papadopoulos met Australian diplomat Alexander Downer for drinks at a high-end London bar called the Kensington Wine Rooms. Little is known about how this meeting came about, but the contrast between the two men could hardly have been starker. Downer, a spry sixty-four years old, was a seasoned politician who had held senior leadership posts in the Australian government for more than two decades. Papadopoulos could barely be described as an upstart. Before signing on with Donald Trump in March 2016, his sole political experience had been two months of service on the ramshackle Ben Carson campaign. Nevertheless, the two men apparently spoke long enough for Papadopoulos to become inebriated and boast about his knowledge of Russia's stolen emails. When Wikileaks released hacked Democratic National Committee emails two months later, Australian officials relayed the substance of this conversation to the FBI.[21]

A True First-Rate Professional

Back in the United States, parallel events were unfolding almost simultaneously. On March 29, with virtually no vetting, Donald Trump hired longtime lobbyist, lawyer, and political consultant Paul Manafort as his convention manager. At this point, many Republican elites remained deeply uncomfortable with Trump. As a result, the candidate and his advisors were increasingly worried about the possibility of a delegate revolt on the floor of the Republican convention. Manafort seemed just the sort of experienced hand required to manage such a scenario. Upon learning of his appointment, veteran Republican lobbyist Vin Weber gushed: "he's one of the true first-rate professionals in the Republican Party. There's only a handful of people, I really mean that, that can honestly say they know how a national convention works. He's one of them."[22]

The reality was far more interesting—and complicated. Nearing seventy, with a full head of brown hair and a conspicuous chin dimple, Paul Manafort might have stepped straight out of a John LeCarré novel. As a young protege of James A. Baker III, Manafort had wrangled delegates for Gerald Ford in 1976, successfully blunting a convention floor challenge by the insurgent Ronald Reagan. Later, in the early 1980s, Manafort shrewdly helped to pioneer the marriage of lobbying and political consulting. This fusion dramatically increased the influence of special interests in Washington and made Manafort himself a wealthy man. Such conventional success, however, could never satisfy Paul Manafort.[23]

A man of extraordinary appetites and restless ambition, Manafort soon grasped the potential for even greater riches and excitement in the new frontier of foreign lobbying. By the mid-1990s, he had worked on behalf of dictatorships in nearly a dozen countries, including the Philippines, Nigeria, Saudi Arabia, and Zaire. He had also begun to moonlight as a major broker of international arms deals in partnership with the famed Lebanese arms dealer Abdul Rahman Al-Assir. It was this career trajectory, and the need to support an ever more opulent lifestyle, that landed Manafort in his last major job before joining the Trump campaign—as chief political strategist to Victor Yanukovich, the Russian-backed president of Ukraine.[24]

This position brought with it vast wealth and power and a complex web of foreign financial entanglements. Among those entanglements was an $18.9 million debt to the notoriously ruthless

Russian oligarch Oleg Deripaska. When Yanukovich was forced to flee Ukraine during the Euromaidan Revolution of February 2014, Manafort's entire house of cards came crashing down. Suddenly, cash was tight. New clients were not forthcoming. Amid this upheaval, the exposure of an extended extramarital affair in November 2014 sent Manafort into an emotional downward spiral. By the spring of 2015, he had checked himself into an inpatient rehabilitation center in Arizona. His twenty-nine-year-old daughter Andrea worried that her father was in the midst of "a massive emotional breakdown." Joining the Trump campaign was supposed to be the first step in his personal and professional resurrection.[25]

Despite his severe cash flow problems, Manafort agreed to work for free. Partly this seems to have been based on his perceptive intuition that Trump was, despite his enormous wealth, cheap. He also thought that Trump would respect him more if he did not appear to need the money. Most important, Manafort seems to have believed that his work on the campaign could ultimately be leveraged into cash, especially if Trump won the election. Whatever salary he might have commanded as a campaign advisor would pale compared to the value of having the president's ear.[26]

His attempts to cash in began almost immediately. Less than two weeks after joining the campaign, Manafort reached out to Oleg Deripaska, through an intermediary, after dodging him for over two years. "I assume you have shown our friends my media coverage, right?" Manafort wrote by email. "How do we use to get whole? Has OVD operation seen?" "OVD," Manafort later acknowledged, was short for Oleg Vladimir Deripaska, who, like all Russian oligarchs in good standing, was a close ally of Vladimir Putin. On July 7, 2016, Manafort sent a follow-up email, appearing to offer Deripaska personalized and confidential reports on the Trump campaign. "If he needs private briefings, we can accommodate," Manafort wrote. To all appearances, Trump's new campaign chairman was attempting to sell his influence on the Republican presidential candidate to a hostile foreign power.[27]

The Trump Tower Meeting

The story gets even weirder and more surreal. On June 3, 2016, Donald Trump Jr. the Republican candidate's eldest son and senior campaign advisor, received a fateful email. The sender was British music publicist and former tabloid journalist Rob Goldstone. Fleshy-faced and bombastic, with an affinity for goofy hats, Goldstone seemed an unlikely go-between for a high-stakes international power play, but that is just what his message proposed.[28]

According to Goldstone, his principal client, the Azerbaijani pop star Emin Agalarov, had damaging information to pass along about Hillary Clinton. This would seem almost too preposterous to be true, but Agalarov was not just any pop star. He was the son of Aras Agalarov, the billionaire oligarch and Vladimir Putin crony who financed Donald Trump's 2013 Miss Universe pageant in Moscow. Goldstone's email promised "very high level and sensitive information" that "would incriminate Hillary and her dealings with Russia and would be very useful to your father." Lest there be any doubt about the provenance of this information, Goldstone emphasized that it was "part of Russia and its government's support for Mr. Trump."[29]

Trump Jr. was enthusiastic. In words that would later become famous, he quickly wrote back to Goldstone: "if it's what you say I love it." A meeting was set for June 9 at Trump Tower. On June 7, Donald Trump won New Jersey's uncontested Republican primary, having become the party's presumptive nominee a month earlier. That evening, he gave an unusually subdued victory speech at a rally in Westchester County, New York. Roughly seven minutes into the speech, backed by his family and four large, gold-tasseled

American flags, Trump made a teasing announcement. "I am going to give a major speech on, probably, Monday of next week," he said, with a theatrically mischievous grin. "We're going to discuss all of the things that have taken place with the Clintons. I think you're going to find it very, very interesting." Pausing for effect, he added, "I wonder if the press will want to attend. Who knows?"[30]

At 4 p.m. on June 9, Rob Goldstone, three Russians, and a translator were ushered into a conference room on an upper floor of Trump Tower, the gleaming fifty-eight-story skyscraper where Donald Trump maintained his primary residence before moving to the White House. They were joined by Donald Trump Jr.; his brother-in-law and fellow campaign advisor Jared Kushner; and Paul Manafort, who had recently been promoted to campaign chairman. Expectations for the meeting were evidently high. This was virtually the entire brain trust of the Trump presidential campaign as it then stood.[31]

Donald Trump Jr. cut straight to the chase. "I believe you have some information for us," he said. This remark was addressed to Natalia Veselnitskaya, a pretty forty-one-year-old lawyer whom Emin Agalarov had repeatedly described as "highly connected." The discussion that followed remains shrouded in mystery, but the broad outlines are fairly well established.

Veselnitskaya came prepared with a memo detailing allegations of financial misconduct by two Clinton Foundation and Democratic National Committee donors. Her presentation was convoluted, bordering on incomprehensible. But the bottom line was that some of the "stolen money" she described may have been used to finance Hillary Clinton's campaign. More than a year later, compelling evidence would emerge that Veselnitskaya had closely coordinated her message with top officials in Moscow.[32]

In exchange for providing this information, Veselnitskaya urged the Trump team to repeal sanctions the United States had imposed on high-level Russian officials as punishment for human rights abuses. For help making her case, she was joined at the meeting by Rinat Akhmetshin. A flamboyant Russian-American lobbyist and former Soviet counterintelligence officer, Akhmetshin was rumored to have strong ongoing ties to senior Russian intelligence officials. Short, stocky, and bearing a slight resemblance to Rob Goldstone, he would have been hard to miss. According to multiple eyewitnesses, he showed up at the meeting in hot pink jeans and a matching shirt. But Donald Trump Jr. would later deny any recollection of his presence.[33]

The Trump team was unimpressed by Veselnitskaya's pitch. Did she have "any financial documents proving that this money went to Hillary Clinton's campaign?" Donald Trump Jr. asked. She did not, and the conversation petered out in less than half an hour. Veselnitskaya would later describe the meeting as a "failure," but she did not come away totally empty-handed. According to an interview she gave in November 2017, Donald Trump Jr. expressed broad sympathy with her objectives. "Looking ahead, if we come to power, we can return to this issue and think what to do about it," he said, referring to a 2012 sanctions law. "I understand our side may have messed up, but it'll take a long time to get to the bottom of it." Donald Trump never gave his promised speech on the Clintons' dealings with Russia.[34]

All told, members of Trump's campaign team had at least eighteen separate contacts with individuals linked to Vladimir Putin's regime in the seven months preceding the November election. It is normal for presidential candidates to have some contacts with foreign governments. But this extensive pattern of contacts with a hostile foreign power, which Trump and his representatives persistently denied, struck most experienced observers as highly unusual.[35]

Meanwhile, at the personal direction of Vladimir Putin, Russian government agents undertook a comprehensive effort to swing the election in Donald Trump's favor. This campaign encompassed the hacking of the Democratic National Committee's email server and the strategic release of embarrassing emails to coincide with the Democratic National Convention in late July. In the months before the election, Russian agents also penetrated computerized voting systems in roughly twenty states, though they apparently did not change any votes.[36]

Mueller versus Trump

Only after Donald Trump's stunning victory on November 8, 2016, did the American public learn the extent of Russian efforts to swing the election in his favor. The news came fast and furious. Russian cyberattacks on state election systems were widely reported in major media outlets. So was the joint conclusion of federal intelligence agencies that these attacks aimed to help Trump—a conclusion Trump himself stubbornly resisted. During the postelection transition, Trump's nominee for national security advisor was caught on tape promising the Russian ambassador that Trump would ease U.S. sanctions imposed to punish Russian election interference. Most spectacularly of all, the FBI was revealed to have been investigating possible collusion between members of the Trump campaign and the Russian government since late July 2016. That was when Australian diplomat Alexander Downing passed along the substance of his conversation with George Papadopoulos.[37]

In the midst of this deluge, several media outlets reported that Jeff Sessions had misled Congress about his communications with Russia during the presidential campaign. Although it was not immediately apparent, this would prove to be the straw that broke the camel's back. The next day, the flustered and agitated attorney general called a press conference to announce that he would recuse himself from any further involvement in the FBI's ongoing investigation of Russian interference in the presidential campaign.[38]

Two months later, President Trump fired FBI director James Comey under highly irregular circumstances. Comey had come in for significant criticism from both sides during the recent presidential campaign. But the official explanation Trump gave for firing him was that Comey had improperly interfered with the 2016 presidential election to the detriment of *Hillary Clinton*. Two days later, Trump described his actual thought process in a rambling interview with NBC's Lester Holt: "when I decided to just do it, I said to myself, I said 'You know, this Russia thing with Trump and Russia is a made-up story, it's an excuse by the Democrats for having lost an election that they should have won.'" It soon emerged that Trump had previously asked Comey to drop the FBI's investigation of Michael Flynn, his then national security advisor—a request that many legal experts said could constitute obstruction of justice.[39]

Demands to appoint a special prosecutor, which had been building for some months, quickly intensified and gained bipartisan support. With Attorney General Sessions recused, the responsibility for answering those demands fell to deputy attorney general Rod Rosenstein. A sober and mild-mannered career civil servant, Rosenstein had cut his teeth as a junior lawyer in Ken Starr's investigation of Bill Clinton. Surprising many of President Trump's critics and apparently the president himself, Rosenstein promptly appointed Robert Mueller as special counsel. It is difficult to imagine Jeff Sessions, an ardent Trump loyalist, taking this step. This makes the attorney general's recusal and the Russia testimony that precipitated it two of the most consequential events of Trump's presidency.[40]

Rosenstein's order gave Mueller broad authority to investigate any coordination or collusion between the Russian government and Donald Trump's presidential campaign. It also extended that authority to any charges arising directly out of the Russia investigation, specifically including false statements, perjury, and obstruction of justice. This would be the first serious test of the special counsel regulations that Neal Katyal and his colleagues had worked so hard to craft nineteen years earlier.[41]

The initial response to Mueller's appointment was almost universally favorable. A patrician New Yorker who served with distinction in Vietnam, Mueller was an old-fashioned establishment Republican with a long-standing reputation for inflexible integrity. Both Democrats and Republicans lauded his probity, ability, and extensive prosecutorial experience. Even so vocal a Trump partisan as former House speaker Newt Gingrich declared: "Robert Mueller is a superb choice to be special counsel."[42]

Less than a month later, many Republicans began to change their tune. Gingrich was in the vanguard, arguing that "Republicans are delusional if they think the special counsel is going to be fair." He and others pointed to the campaign donations of Mueller's staff and the ostensible friendship between Mueller and former FBI director Comey. Gingrich was particularly rankled by Comey's deliberate leaking of an unclassified memorandum recording Trump's attempted interference with the FBI investigation of Michael Flynn.[43]

As Mueller's investigation picked up steam, so too did Republican attacks. President Trump himself repeatedly and angrily derided the investigation as a "witch hunt" orchestrated by Democrats out of sour grapes. Trump's partisan allies and sympathetic media organs, like Fox News and conservative talk radio, helped to amplify and disseminate this message. The energy and imagination Trump's defenders displayed in this campaign are a testament to human ingenuity and the intensity of modern tribal loyalties. Their attacks on Mueller ranged from alleged partisan bias on his prosecutorial team to a deep state conspiracy against President Trump to fuzzy allegations of collusion between Russia and Hillary Clinton to alleged abuse of foreign intelligence wiretaps and FBI informants. None of these charges held up to serious scrutiny, but cumulatively they had a significant effect on Mueller's credibility, especially among Republicans.[44]

President Trump apparently tried to fire Mueller in June 2017 but backed down when White House Counsel Donald McGahn threatened to resign. Subsequently, Trump launched a barrage of unprecedented public attacks on Jeff Sessions, apparently hoping to humiliate him into resigning. This would have enabled Trump to appoint a new attorney general who might be persuaded to fire Mueller. It would also have saved Trump the dirty work—and the political fallout—of actually firing Sessions or Rosenstein.

This is much how special prosecutor investigations have always worked. Political pressure forced Trump to acquiesce in the appointment of a genuinely independent special counsel. This gave Trump and his allies powerful political incentives to attack Mueller, which they did with ruthless ferocity. For special prosecutors, that is par for the course. For the American people, it is cause for intense vigilance.[45]

PART II Law

6

Can the President Be Charged with a Crime?

During the 2016 presidential campaign, Donald Trump famously quipped that "I could stand in the middle of 5th Avenue and shoot somebody, and I wouldn't lose voters." He was presumably speaking in jest, or at least hyperbolically, but what if a sitting president actually did this? More realistically, what if a sitting president accepted illegal foreign campaign donations or sought to obstruct an ongoing federal investigation? Could he or she be charged with a crime? The conventional wisdom is no, but the Constitution is silent on this question, no court has ever decided it, and there are respectable arguments on both sides.[1]

The principal argument that a sitting president cannot be charged with a crime is based on the impeachment clause of the U.S. Constitution. That clause provides that a president—or any other official—who has been removed from office by impeachment "shall nevertheless be liable and subject to Indictment, Trial, Judgement, and Punishment, according to Law." By explicitly permitting the president to be charged with a crime *after* he is removed from office, this language seems to imply that the president cannot be charged with a crime *before* he is removed.

Those who take this view generally bolster their textual argument with a practical argument. The president, they contend, exercises unique—and uniquely important—responsibilities in our constitutional system. If a sitting president could be charged with a crime, his ability to discharge those responsibilities effectively might be severely hampered. It is virtually impossible to imagine the president running the federal government and conducting U.S. foreign policy from jail. But if sitting presidents can be charged with a crime, they can presumably be convicted and sentenced. In such a case, the president might well end up incarcerated. Even if that complication could be avoided, perhaps by mandatory bail, the essential problem would remain. The cloud of uncertainty and opprobrium carried by criminal charges would badly, perhaps fatally, weaken any president facing indictment or conviction. Such an outcome would seem to frustrate the framers' decision to place the impeachment power in the hands of Congress, rather than the courts.

These are plausible arguments, but there are also strong arguments on the other side. The principle that no one is above the law runs deep in the American tradition. If the president cannot be charged with a crime, that would place him above the law in an important sense. The Constitution nowhere explicitly mandates this outcome. Many distinguished lawyers and commentators have argued that we should not lightly infer a rule so much at odds with basic American values. The founders, after all, fought a war rather than submit to the principle that "the King can do no wrong."

There is more. The impeachment clause of the Constitution makes no distinction between presidents and other federal officials, such as judges and cabinet officers. If the president cannot be charged with a crime, the same rule would seem to govern the secretary of defense, the attorney general, and federal judges. Yet there are many historical examples of such officials, especially judges, being charged with crimes. Even Richard Nixon's vice president, Spiro Agnew, was charged with—and ultimately pled guilty to—tax evasion while still in office. Absent any contrary indication in the constitutional text, why should the president be treated differently?

This question is an urgent one for special prosecutors investigating the president because it determines their endgame. If the president can be charged with a crime, a special prosecutor's goal is to determine whether the evidence warrants this extraordinary step. If the president cannot be charged with a crime, the special prosecutor's goals are less clear. But historically, they have included developing a factual record on which Congress might base an impeachment decision. Either way, the legal questions are shot through with politics. Because there is no clearly established law on point, any special prosecutor deciding whether to pursue charges against the president must consider whether the country—or the president—will stand for it. Seldom has any one person, other than a president himself, faced a decision with greater consequences for the nation.

A Tense Internal Debate

Leon Jaworski succeeded Archibald Cox as Watergate special prosecutor on November 5, 1973. It was immediately apparent that the two men had very different personal and managerial styles. Cox was cerebral, high-minded, and professorial. He liked to talk through major decisions with his subordinates in the egalitarian fashion of a New England town meeting. Jaworski, a bulky Texan with a large head of receding white hair, was much more a man of the world. His primary experience was not in the rarefied atmosphere of the Supreme Court but down in the trenches of the Texas trial courts. By temperament and philosophy, he was a pragmatist.

He believed in getting things done and had little patience for extended debate. While nominally a Democrat, he was known to be a strong political conservative.[2]

Jaworski faced a considerable challenge in taking over the sprawling Watergate investigation midstream. The terms of his appointment gave him "complete freedom" to select his own team. But as a practical matter, he had little choice but to retain the staff of roughly forty lawyers that Cox had recruited and hired. Those lawyers were nearly all Ivy League–educated easterners a full generation younger than Jaworski. They came from an entirely different cultural and professional world than their new boss, who had graduated from Baylor Law School and spent virtually his whole life in Texas. They had also been deeply shaken by the trauma of the Saturday Night Massacre. Few believed that Nixon would appoint anyone but a reliable stooge to replace Cox. When Jaworski addressed them for the first time at the 1425 K Street offices on the afternoon of November 5, the air was thick with mutual mistrust.[3]

Three months later, relations between Jaworski and his staff remained chilly, remote, and somewhat tense. As January 1974 came to a close, the young Watergate Task Force lawyers began the work of drafting an indictment. The defendants would include Richard Nixon's top advisors. The principal charge would be conspiracy to obstruct justice by covering up the Watergate burglary. The evidence was overwhelming, and the president was right at the heart of it, but no one knew quite how to handle this. Could the special prosecutor indict the president? If not, what else could be done? In late January and early February, the task force lawyers talked of little else, but they knew that Jaworksi himself would have to make the final call, and he had said nothing at all on the subject to the lawyers responsible for drafting the indictment.[4]

This was not because Jaworski was not interested or concerned. The question weighed on him heavily, but he was still leery of his aggressive young team of prosecutors. Loyalty counted greatly with Jaworski, and he was not yet certain how far he could count on the loyalty of his staff. He therefore commissioned a top-secret analysis from Philip Lacovara, head of the legal research team.

A slightly pudgy, mustachioed veteran of the solicitor general's office, Lacovara had graduated first in his class from Columbia Law School. As a government lawyer, he had quickly earned a reputation for legal brilliance, but he did not immediately apply his talents to the question at hand. Instead, he delegated the assignment to a junior lawyer, who cautiously doubted the "propriety" of indicting the president. Unsatisfied, Lacovara drafted his own supplementary memorandum emphasizing that "there was no explicit or *implicit* constitutional bar to indictment." In an earlier analysis for Archibald Cox, Harvard law professor John Hart Ely—perhaps the greatest constitutional law scholar in U.S. history—had reached the same conclusion.[5]

Jaworski remained deeply skeptical. Constitutional niceties aside, he could not imagine hauling the president into court like a common criminal. What if he refused to comply? What if there was a nuclear war? Would the president just ask for a recess? Jaworski seriously doubted whether the president could perform his constitutional functions while under indictment. Besides, indicting the president would mean endless delays as the inevitable legal challenges worked their way through the courts. Meanwhile, the president's lawyers and public relations people would pound the special prosecutor's office in the court of public opinion. All this would complicate Jaworski's ability to prosecute the other major players in the conspiracy. There were just too many downsides.[6]

A Risky Memorandum

By the first week of February, Jaworski's continuing silence had pushed several younger members of his staff into a state of active alarm. Was it possible that he meant to take no action at all regarding the president? Murmurings to this effect spread through the office like a virus. George Frampton, one of Archibald Cox's first hires, and a few others decided that they had to act. They could not allow Jaworski to make such a momentous decision without at least putting their views to him in writing. Together, they drafted a memorandum making the case for indictment.[7]

It was, they recognized, a risky move. Jaworski was obviously sensitive about handling the president, and he did not take it well when others challenged his judgment. To make matters worse, he might regard their memo as an aggressive, even hostile, maneuver. It might look like they were trying to put themselves on the record so they could criticize his decision later. The memo they produced clearly reflects these anxieties. Alternately strident and deferential, it reads as a plaintive, impassioned, almost poignant, plea to the effect of "we really think the President can be indicted, but even if you disagree, please do *something*."[8]

The memo begins by emphasizing the special prosecutor's duty and responsibility to "investigate and *prosecute* allegations involving the President." It explains the importance of this duty to restoring public confidence in the government. This, the memo repeatedly points out, was the whole rationale for appointing a special prosecutor in the first place. The memo also emphasizes the unique constitutional role of the grand jury, which the special prosecutor would soon ask to hand down indictments.

This group of ordinary men and women had given two years of their lives to the Watergate investigation. All of them had sworn an oath to make a "true presentment" of "all offenses" that came to their knowledge. Could the special prosecutor in good conscience ask these dedicated citizens to do anything less in the case of the president? "For us or the grand jury to shirk from an appropriate expression of our honest assessment of the President's guilt," the young lawyers wrote, "would not only be a departure from our responsibilities but a dangerous precedent damaging to the rule of law."[9]

Finally, the memo reaches its central point: "there is nothing in the text or the legislative history of the Constitution that bars indictment of a sitting President." Conceding that several "political considerations" might weigh against indictment, the memo systematically works through these arguments and finds all of them wanting. Its most interesting claim is that indicting the president would be no more disruptive than impeachment proceedings and probably less. A criminal trial, the memo points out, would be relatively short and focused on a few discrete charges precisely defined by law. Impeachment proceedings could last months, would lack well-established norms or procedures, and would likely be premised on comparatively hazy charges and evidence. If the impasse created by indictment or conviction of the president proved intolerable, impeachment gave Congress and the people a ready remedy.[10]

While pressing the case for indictment vigorously, the memo carefully stops short of insisting on that course. Frampton and his coauthors knew that Jaworski would ultimately make that decision for himself. They also felt that their chances of persuading him to their view were relatively slim. The memo, therefore, bends over backward to defer to Jaworski's judgment on these questions.

More important than this stylistic deference, the memo offered Jaworski a concrete alternative—the now obscure but historically well-pedigreed device of "presentment." Basically, presentment would permit the grand jury to formally declare that "if he were not President, Richard Nixon would have been indicted." In this way, the grand jury and the special prosecutor could uphold the rule of law while avoiding the most pressing practical objections to indictment. With the judge's permission, the grand jury could also refer a presentment to Congress for use in impeachment proceedings. It was still a grave step to accuse the president of the United States of a crime, but the memo's authors thought that step necessary to safeguard "the force of law in our social and governmental processes."[11]

An Explosion Breaks the Ice

Frampton submitted the memo to Jaworski on February 12 to spectacular effect. Jaworski was not merely unpersuaded; he felt blindsided and betrayed. Previously, he had been "bothered by feelings that the task force was too eager to take on the White House at every opportunity." Now, he seemed to have "a mutiny on his hands." At a meeting the next day, Jaworski exploded in anger at Richard Ben-Veniste, the cocksure and irreverent young chief of the Watergate task force. Clearly, Ben-Veniste had put Frampton and the others up to writing the memo as "frontmen" for himself. The task force lawyers, Jaworski said, were trying to sow discord in the office "in order to limit his freedom of action."[12]

This blowup left staff morale in shambles. Jaworski was not merely uninterested in their input; he seemed to regard them as "virtual renegades." In retrospect, however, this confrontation marked an important turning point. In the days that followed, the task force lawyers regrouped and talked among themselves about how to proceed. Gradually, they opened up constructive lines of communication with Jaworski, who proved himself more open-minded than he had initially appeared.[13]

It helped that all of the parties were strongly motivated to solve the same thorny practical problem: How do you prosecute a conspiracy to obstruct justice without prosecuting its ringleader? Every first-year law student learns that members of a criminal conspiracy are liable for the acts of all other members taken to further the conspiracy. This meant that Nixon's aides were liable for the criminal acts of the president as well as their own. But first prosecutors would have to establish that all were knowing members of the same conspiracy. How were they to do that without indicting or even seeking a presentment against Nixon?

There was, however, an even bigger problem. Much of the best evidence against Nixon's aides came from the White House tapes that the president had turned over after the Saturday Night Massacre. But in general, such out-of-court statements qualify as hearsay. That makes them inadmissible in court under the Federal Rules of Evidence. Those rules make an exception for the statements of coconspirators, but to take advantage of that exception, the prosecution would need to establish that the president fit this description.[14]

These were hardly novel problems. In many conspiracy prosecutions, one or more members of the conspiracy cannot be indicted due to legal immunity, mental incompetence, or death. In such cases, prosecutors can name these individuals as "unindicted coconspirators." This enables their actions to be held against the indicted members of the conspiracy. It also allows their out-of-court statements to be admitted in evidence under the "coconspirator exception" to the hearsay rules.

Jaworski, however, was adamantly opposed to taking any step that could be construed as accusing the president of a crime. In his mind, asking the grand jury to name the president an unindicted coconspirator was no different from asking it to issue a presentment against him. Both would cast a pall of opprobrium over the presidency. Both would also bring down the full weight of the president's wrath on the special prosecutor's office. On the other hand, as an experienced trial lawyer, Jaworksi keenly understood the difficulties his position created for the prosecution of

Nixon's aides. And he cared about that prosecution as deeply as his staffers did.[15]

Over the last two weeks in February, the task force lawyers hit upon an ingenious solution to this dilemma. What if the special prosecutor asked the grand jury to vote *now* to authorize him to name the president as an unindicted coconspirator *later*? As Frampton and Ben-Veniste later recalled, this approach would solve the trial-related problems that worried the young prosecutors. It would also satisfy Jaworski's "strong desire to avoid public confrontation with the President. When it became necessary to name the President, Jaworski could defend that action by arguing that it was a prerequisite to effective prosecution of Nixon's aides." Jaworski liked the idea and asked Ben-Veniste to put it in writing.[16]

The Bulging Briefcase

Figuring out what to do about the president was not the only thorny problem on the special prosecutor's hands. Jaworski and his team were also wrestling with the equally thorny question of what the grand jury could report to Congress and how. In ruling out presentment, Jaworski had made clear that he would not sign off on any strategy that accused the president of a crime. He remained open to sending evidence to Congress, including the highly incriminating White House tapes. But he strongly opposed appending any summary, analysis, or "theory of the case" against the president. Raw evidence, he thought, would speak for itself. Anything else might subject the grand jury to criticism for overstepping its role. Jaworski also worried that Judge Sirica, the stern former pugilist who presided over the grand jury proceeding, would balk at any accusatory report.[17]

The young task force lawyers did not share Jaworski's concerns. They believed that an accusatory approach was amply supported by historical precedent. They were also deeply concerned about the prospect of transmitting raw evidence. The House Judiciary Committee, which would ultimately vote on impeachment, was already awash in more evidence than it could make sense of. This left plenty of room for the president's defenders to maneuver. Without firm guidance from the special prosecutor, there seemed a real risk that the Committee's investigation would break down into inconclusive partisan bickering. Far more than evidence, the young lawyers thought, the Committee needed guidance, summary, and synthesis.[18]

Jaworski had firmly rejected summary and analysis, but the task force lawyers were not prepared to give up. Perhaps there was a "middle course" to be found. Without summarizing or analyzing the evidence, the grand jury might be able to "arrange it in a format that made its significance as clear as possible. Even better, the jury could supply the House Judiciary Committee with an index to the evidence showing how various pieces fitted together." The special prosecutor's team would, of course, assist in this effort. The task force lawyers called this approach "the road map." On February 18, the boyish, clean-cut George Frampton and a few others met with Jaworski to make their pitch. The special prosecutor did not say yes, but he did not say no either.[19]

This was enough for Frampton, who began the monumental task of assembling the relevant evidence. Working with other members of the task force, he also began drafting a road map to accompany the evidence. The approach they settled on was simple and clean. The road map would comprise a series of spare "Statements of Fact," each followed by a list of supporting evidence. This format was chosen to satisfy Jaworski's exacting conditions, though Ben-Veniste and Frampton later acknowledged their hope that it would "serve as a do-it-yourself kit for the Judiciary Committee, helping it reassemble the individual pieces of grand jury testimony and other evidence into a coherent theory of a criminal case."[20]

The special prosecutor was scheduled to address the grand jury at 10 a.m. on February 25. As of that morning, the task force lawyers still did not know what he had decided about the road map or about secretly naming Richard Nixon as an unindicted conspirator. When Jaworski arrived at the office, Frampton was the only lawyer there. Jaworski handed him a sheaf of papers and asked him to have the task force secretary type them up. "It's what I am going to tell the grand jury," Jaworski said drily.[21]

Frampton waited for the special prosecutor to leave his office and raced through the handwritten pages he had been handed. Jaworski had embraced both of his staffers' proposals. He would seek the grand jury's authorization to include the president on a list of unindicted coconspirators, who would be named publicly "at a later date." He would also tell the jury that it could "transmit evidence to the House Judiciary Committee by way of a report, and the prosecutors would assist in this task in any way desired by the jurors."[22]

Later that morning, Leon Jaworski arrived at the E. Barrett Prettyman Courthouse to address the grand jury. Many jurors asked pointed questions about his suggestion that they could not indict the president. But Jaworski defended his position capably and apparently persuasively. After fielding questions, he left the task force lawyers to present the draft indictment and proposed list of conspirators. The jurors then retired to deliberate privately. When they returned, Vladimir Pregelj, the impassive, goateed forty-six-year-old foreman, announced their decision. They had voted nineteen to zero to name the president as an unindicted coconspirator.[23]

It still remained for the task force lawyers to complete the road map and assemble the supporting evidence for the jury's approval.

They worked frantically to meet Jaworski's self-imposed March 1 deadline. By Thursday, February 28, both the indictment and road map were complete. That evening, Frampton carefully assembled the assorted tapes and documents referenced in the road map. He then packed them into an oversize brown case, which would soon become known from press reports as "the bulging briefcase." They all fit, but just barely.

The next morning, Jaworski and his team rode the back elevator to Judge Sirica's small, second-story courtroom, along with the grand jury. Imposing and vaguely funereal in his long black robe, Judge Sirica entered and called the proceedings to order. Jaworski sat behind the same walnut counsel table where Archibald Cox had defended his subpoena of Nixon's White House tapes just six months earlier. At Sirica's signal, Jaworski rose and explained that "the grand jury had material to be delivered to the court." As foreman Vladimir Pregelj strode forward from the first row of spectator benches, the atmosphere in the courtroom was hushed and expectant. Pregelj passed two large envelopes up to Sirica, one containing the indictment and the other the road map. He then returned to his seat.

Brandishing a formidable letter opener, whose theatrical potential he exploited with deadpan relish, Sirica briskly sliced open both envelopes. When he appeared to be done examining their contents, the equally theatrical Richard Ben-Veniste produced a large brown briefcase from under the counsel table. He walked briskly to the front of the courtroom and hoisted the heavy case to the bench like an offering on the altar. Sirica accepted it without comment.

Sometimes discretion is the better part of valor. Jaworski and his team had not indicted the president, but they had given the House Judiciary Committee a road map to impeachment. They had also ensured that the country would learn, eventually, that a grand jury had found probable cause to accuse Richard Nixon of a crime. The events of March 1, 1974, in Judge Sirica's courtroom went a long way toward forcing Nixon to resign in disgrace the following August. In this way, Leon Jaworski accomplished the same result his young lieutenants hoped to accomplish through indictment or presentment. He helped the American people vindicate the principle "that no man in this country is so high as to be above the law."

Once More unto the Breach

In the waning days of January 1999, President William Jefferson Clinton seemed increasingly certain to survive his Senate impeachment trial. The president's polished, professional lawyers were running circles around the inept congressmen—called "managers"—who served as impeachment prosecutors. Several procedural votes narrowly won by the president's Republican adversaries demonstrated the cold truth. They were very far from mustering the two-thirds majority required to convict and remove Clinton from office. Everywhere he went, the president impressed those around him with the renewed spring in his step. Then he read the January 31 edition of the *New York Times*.[24]

Splashed across the front page was the headline "Starr Is Weighing Whether to Indict Sitting President." The story explained that Independent Counsel Ken Starr had solicited outside legal advice from two conservative constitutional law professors. Both advised him that "the Constitution and legal precedent provide a prosecutor with the authority to seek the indictment, trial and conviction of a sitting President." According to anonymous "associates," Starr agreed with this view. But he had not decided "whether, or when, to ask the grand jury to charge Mr. Clinton with perjury and obstruction of justice in the Monica S. Lewinsky matter."[25]

The backstory was strikingly similar to the one that transpired in the Watergate special prosecutor's office almost precisely twenty-five years earlier. A group of hard-charging young prosecutors in Starr's office was convinced that Bill Clinton had committed indictable offenses. They thought they could persuade an impartial jury to convict and were eager to get started. To that end, they were pressing Starr to seek a grand jury indictment of Clinton immediately after the Senate impeachment trial. Starr's staffers were familiar with the memorandum George Frampton and others had written to Leon Jaworski, which they passed around like samizdat. As a group, they enthusiastically endorsed its conclusion: "a failure to indict the incumbent President, in the face of evidence of his criminal activity, would seriously impair the integrity of the criminal process."[26]

As had been the case in the Watergate special prosecutor's office, many of Ken Starr's most eager subordinates were in their late twenties or early thirties. But the generation gap between the staff and the special prosecutor was not quite so large. In 1974, Leon Jaworski was sixty-nine. In 1999, Starr was only fifty-three. Perhaps in part for this reason, Starr was more receptive than Jaworski to arguments that the Constitution permitted him to indict a sitting president.[27]

The arguments pressed by Starr's experts and staff lawyers closely paralleled the arguments Jaworski had rejected as unwise and impractical. The Constitution nowhere explicitly grants a sitting president immunity against criminal prosecution. This could not be a mere oversight because the framers knew how to grant such immunity when they wanted to. The speech or debate clause exempts members of Congress from criminal prosecution for anything said or done during legislative debates. The framers could have granted a similar exemption to the president but chose not to. Practical arguments for inferring such an exemption were unpersuasive. Indictment of a sitting president would no more "cripple the presidency" than would impeachment, which the framers apparently thought perfectly tolerable.[28]

Ken Starr's constitutional expert Ronald Rotunda also advanced two new arguments. A former Democrat, Rotunda had worked for the Senate Watergate Committee right out of Harvard Law School. Over the years, he had evolved into a staunch conservative with close ties to the Heritage Foundation, the Federalist Society, and other bastions of the legal right. By 1999, no one knowledgeable about constitutional law was surprised to see him working for Ken Starr or supporting the indictment of a sitting Democratic president. Nevertheless, Rotunda's Watergate bona fides gave him a certain gravitas, as did his long and distinguished record as a scholar.[29]

Still, the new arguments Rotunda advanced were weak. First, he contended that the independent counsel statute gave Ken Starr greater constitutional authority than earlier special prosecutors, who were mere creatures of the executive branch. Second, he argued that the Supreme Court's 1996 decision in the Paula Jones case changed everything. By allowing a civil sexual harassment suit against the president, the Court had implicitly negated any argument for a presidential exemption from criminal indictment.[30]

The problem with the first argument is that, constitutionally speaking, Ken Starr remained an "inferior officer" subordinate to the president. In this sense, which was the only relevant one, independent counsels were just like earlier special prosecutors. More important, nothing about the independent counsel's statutory independence lessened the impact a criminal indictment would have on the president's ability to do his job, which is by far the most powerful argument against the constitutionality of indicting a sitting president.[31]

The problem with Rotunda's second argument is its implausible assumption that a criminal indictment would interfere with the president's responsibilities no more than a civil suit would. In retrospect, the Supreme Court was obviously wrong in predicting that a civil sexual harassment suit would not significantly distract the president from his duties. But even if that prediction had proven correct, the Court said nothing to suggest that it would extend to a criminal indictment. It is easy to see why. The opprobrium commonly associated with criminal charges is far greater. So is the imperative for a criminal defendant to participate personally in his own defense. The Supreme Court might someday extend its Paula Jones decision to the criminal indictment of a sitting president, but that possibility seems quite remote. In any case, Rotunda's confident assertions on this point were unsupported and unpersuasive.[32]

Whatever their merits, Rotunda's arguments evidently persuaded Ken Starr. Perhaps he wanted to be persuaded. He had devoted nearly five years of his life to investigating and prosecuting Bill Clinton. As a purely psychological matter, it must have been extraordinarily difficult to watch the Republican impeachment effort peter out in the Senate. Even worse, to some of Starr's subordinates, was the spectacular hypocrisy and arrogance—as they saw it—of the president's lawyers. They reserved special scorn for the president's lead attorney, David Kendall. At several points during Clinton's trial, Kendall pointedly suggested that charges of perjury and obstruction of justice more properly belonged in a courtroom. Was this a taunt? A dare? Perhaps an invitation?[33]

Ultimately, Starr resisted the temptation to pursue his white whale any further. He has never explained this decision publicly. But privately, Starr indicated that his decision "would be guided by a number of factors, including the impact that an indictment of the President would have on the nation and the Government." In practical terms, the decision to seek an indictment is ultimately the decision to remove—or at least critically disable—a duly elected president. Perhaps Ken Starr eventually came to recognize that such an essentially political decision is better entrusted to an elected body like Congress.[34] This had been Leon Jaworski's view from the beginning. Whatever his motive, Starr's restraint after Clinton's Senate acquittal had the salutary effect of ceding final authority to the American people and their representatives.

Alternate Endgames

Future special prosecutors will likely follow the same course. For one thing, there is much practical wisdom behind it. Presidents have an extraordinarily difficult job even under the best of circumstances. It is hard to imagine a president doing that job effectively while under indictment, much less after suffering a criminal conviction. At a minimum, it seems dangerous to empower an unelected special prosecutor—or a randomly selected grand jury—to wield such power. There is also the simple fact that the president can fire a special prosecutor. The costs of exercising this power are normally high, but they are unlikely to exceed the costs of suffering a criminal indictment. Any special prosecutor who pursues this course is unlikely to have a job for long. Knowing this, most special prosecutors are likely to look long and hard for a more palatable alternative.

The special counsel regulations adopted in 2000 supply another reason to doubt that future special prosecutors will seek to indict a sitting president. Those regulations require special counsels to comply with all "rules, regulations, procedures, practices and policies of the Justice Department." This is generally understood to include the "controlling" legal opinions of the Office of Legal Counsel, which has twice concluded that a sitting president cannot be indicted.

The regulations do permit a special counsel to seek an exemption from Justice Department policies in "extraordinary circumstances." But the attorney general—or acting attorney general, if the attorney general is recused—would need to sign off. Like a special counsel, however, the Attorney General can be fired by the president. This means that two high officials would have to disregard their natural instinct for self-preservation. That is certainly possible but does not seem likely to happen often.[35]

This does not mean that special prosecutors are powerless to hold the president accountable for violating the law. The approaches debated by the Watergate task force illustrate some tools that remain at a special prosecutor's disposal even if indictment is off the table. Most obviously, a special prosecutor might ask the grand jury to name the president as an unindicted coconspirator, just as Leon Jaworski did with Richard Nixon. This would signal that a group of randomly selected citizens found probable cause to believe that the president had committed a crime.

Current Justice Department policies discourage the practice of naming unindicted coconspirators, but this policy is not a categorical prohibition. It is a general rule that applies only "in the absence of some significant justification." With indictment off the table, a special prosecutor might well determine that public accountability justifies naming the president as an unindicted coconspirator. Unlike an ordinary citizen, the president has vast resources at his disposal for responding to the public stigma this would entail. On the other hand that stigma might have some of the same downsides as an indictment.[36]

A special prosecutor might also ask the grand jury to issue a presentment formally accusing the president of a crime. This could be issued publicly or transmitted secretly to Congress for consideration of impeachment. Less drastically, the special prosecutor could ask the jury to transmit a purely factual report to

Congress, along with supporting evidence. Both of these actions have historical precedents, including the actions of the Watergate grand jury. But both might violate the rule requiring special prosecutors to provide a "confidential report" to the attorney general at the close of their investigation. Least controversially, a special prosecutor could simply submit a secret report to the attorney general detailing the evidence against the president. Political pressure might well compel the attorney general to make such a report public. Congress could also attempt to obtain it by subpoena. This alternative, unlike the others, is specifically contemplated by the special counsel regulations.[37]

In all these scenarios, the American people have a central—and daunting—role to play. It is not enough for the people to protect a special prosecutor from interference or removal by a self-interested president. Public pressure must also force Congress to hold the president accountable. The only constitutional mechanism provided for this purpose is the arduous process of impeachment. To remove a president from office requires a simple majority vote in the House of Representatives and a two-thirds majority in the Senate. Needless to say, this is a tall order. No American president has ever been removed by impeachment, though Richard Nixon probably would have been had he not resigned first.

To make matters worse, Congress will often be controlled by the president's own political party. On the other hand if legislators put party over principle, they can be held accountable at the voting booth. Once again, the last, best hope for the rule of law is not judges or lawyers but democratic politics.

7

Can the President Be Compelled to Testify under Oath?

It is challenging enough for prosecutors to get an ordinary witness to talk. When the witness is the president of the United States or a close presidential advisor, the challenge reaches a different order of magnitude. The same goes for persuading these officials to produce confidential documents, records, or other physical evidence. Access to such testimony and evidence is essential if special prosecutors are to do their job effectively. But unsurprisingly, presidents and their advisors have not usually been eager to cooperate.

In an ordinary criminal investigation, this problem has a ready solution. Courts can simply order a witness to testify. They can also order any person who possesses relevant evidence to hand it over for inspection. These powers are rooted in a centuries-old principle that "the public has a right to every man's evidence." The logic behind this principle is simple and appealing. Since we all benefit from a trustworthy judicial system, we are all obligated to supply the information that system needs to generate reliable outcomes.[1]

The principle is not absolute, however. Attorneys cannot be forced to testify about confidential communications with their clients or to produce documentary records of those communications. Priests cannot be compelled to disclose secrets revealed to them during confession. Faced with demands for testimony or evidence, presidents have often argued that their private communications should be subject to a similar rule. This doctrine is known as "executive privilege," and it is frequently the bane of a special prosecutor's existence.[2]

The standard argument for executive privilege is very similar to the arguments for attorney-client and clergy-penitent privilege. To do their job effectively, presidents require the candid advice of their close advisors. They are less likely to receive such advice if it is subject to compulsory disclosure in court. Presidents also must be able to deliberate freely. To do so, they must be free to consider the widest possible array of options when making important decisions that affect the whole nation. This freedom might be compromised if presidents or their advisors could be compelled to testify under oath about internal executive-branch deliberations. Finally, the presidency is an extraordinarily demanding job that requires great sensitivity to public opinion. If presidents or their advisors could be frequently or lightly forced to testify in public, that would make it much more difficult for them to carry out their vital responsibilities.[3]

These considerations are serious and weighty. The need for some form of executive privilege is almost universally recognized. The devil is in the details. No constitutional or statutory text speaks to the issue, and there are very few helpful judicial decisions. Only one executive privilege dispute has made it all the way to the Supreme Court, and the Court's decision left much room for debate. Most executive privilege disputes are resolved by the parties, through negotiation, and not by the courts. In the background of every such negotiation, a single question looms larger than all the rest: What will the American people stand for?[4]

Showdown at the Supreme Court

On the evening of July 7, 1974, a diverse and colorfully dressed crowd gathered beneath the marble portico of the United States Supreme Court. By 9 a.m. the next day, more than a thousand people packed the forty-four marble steps leading up to the court-house entrance. The crowd spilled out in both directions along First Street NE. Roughly two hundred people had waited there all night, but only 136 would receive the tickets they had lined up for. Many of those would be too bleary-eyed to appreciate the historic event they came to see.[5]

Located immediately behind the Capitol at 1 First Street, the Supreme Court is normally a fairly sleepy place in July. By tradition, the justices begin a summer-long recess at the end of June and do not resume their business until October. This, however, was an extraordinary occasion. Watergate special prosecutor Leon Jaworski had subpoenaed sixty-four secret tape recordings of President Richard Nixon talking with his closest advisors. The president had moved to quash—that is, void or suppress—the subpoena, but presiding judge John Sirica had refused to do so. To avoid a time-consuming appellate process, Jaworski had requested immediate Supreme Court review, even though he had prevailed in the lower court. The justices granted this request and scheduled a special summer session to consider the case.[6]

At issue was the fundamental constitutional question: Can a court order the president to produce evidence for an ongoing criminal proceeding? A decision in Nixon's favor would go a long way toward placing the president above the law. A decision in favor of the special prosecutor would reaffirm the fundamental principle memorably captured by Bob Dylan: "even the President of the United States sometimes must have to stand naked." A decision for the special prosecutor would also risk a full-blown constitutional crisis. In recent days, White House spokesmen had conspicuously refused to say whether the president would obey the Supreme Court's decision. With the House Judiciary Committee scheduled to begin debate on impeachment at the end of July, the stakes could not have been much higher.[7]

Arriving at the Court that morning to represent the president was veteran Boston trial lawyer James St. Clair. Sleepy-eyed, gap-toothed, and supremely self-confident, St. Clair had joined Nixon's legal team on the final day of 1973. A partner at the storied law firm of Hale and Dorr, St. Clair was a master of preparation and a reputed "wizard in the courtroom." Like Leon Jaworski, however, his principal experience was in the intensely practical world of state and federal trial courts. He had little experience in Washington and even less arguing appeals—a far more intellectual exercise. He had never argued a case before the United States Supreme Court.[8]

At just past 9 a.m., a nondescript sedan pulled up in front of the Supreme Court. Out of the car stepped Philip Lacovara and Leon Jaworski, by now one of the most recognizable public figures in the country. The crowd erupted in cheers. A Supreme Court veteran, Lacovara wore the black morning coat with vest and tails customary for government lawyers arguing before the justices. The jowly Jaworski wore a dignified navy blue suit. Earlier, Lacovara had protested this deviation from sartorial protocol. In response, the burly Texan special prosecutor wrote him a note: "you should be pleased that I'm not going to show up in cowboy boots and buckskins." As the two men threaded their way through the crowd, someone shouted, "Give 'em hell, Leon baby!"

The three-hour oral argument in *United States v. Nixon* was scheduled to begin at 10 a.m. Jaworski would speak first, followed by St. Clair. Each side would then have an opportunity for rebuttal. Lacovara would do the honors for the special prosecutor's office and St. Clair for the president. Nixon had appointed three of the eight justices who would decide the case. A fourth Nixon appointee, William Rehnquist, recused himself because he had worked closely with John Mitchell, one of the main Watergate defendants.

The stage was set for one of the greatest constitutional and political dramas in American history.

The Back Story

Eight months earlier, Nixon had defused an incipient constitutional crisis by appointing a new special prosecutor after the Saturday Night Massacre. He had also promised to release the eight tapes that Archibald Cox subpoenaed before his dismissal. In the subsequent weeks and months, both the White House and Cox's successor, Leon Jaworski, circled the tapes issue warily. Neither was eager to provoke another high-stakes constitutional showdown if it could be avoided. For the special prosecutor, this meant proceeding slowly and not making any dramatic new attempts to obtain large numbers of tapes. For the president's advisors, it meant signaling openness to compromise. The President would voluntarily provide limited access to the tapes in exchange for the special prosecutor's agreement not to seek further compulsory disclosures. Both sides were reluctant to test the tolerance of the American people.[9]

In December 1973, Nixon's chief of staff, Alexander Haig, invited Jaworski to visit the White House and listen to a handful of tapes. The information Jaworski gleaned from these visits was minimal, but as the son of an evangelical minister, he was content to bide his time as the book of Matthew advised. Then, Nixon abruptly instructed Haig to refuse any further cooperation. Increasingly unstable and paranoid, the president was determined not to be jerked around any longer.[10]

Some special prosecutors might have gone straight to court. But Jaworski responded with an olive branch rather than a subpoena. He and Haig were both reasonable, practical men. Perhaps the president could give the special prosecutor access to one more tape? If so, he might be able to determine, once and for all, which tapes were truly necessary to his work. Jaworski deliberately implied, without explicitly stating, that this could be the key to wrapping up his investigation. If the president provided this one tape, he just might bring the whole nightmare of Watergate to a swift and final conclusion. In the long run, this move would prove a deft bit of lawyering.[11]

The tape in question was from June 4, 1973. On that date, Nixon had unwittingly recorded himself listening to twelve hours of taped conversations with chief prosecution witness John Dean. The president's lawyers had previously reported the tape of at least one crucial conversation with Dean missing. Jaworski's team hoped this "tape of tapes" might include footage of Nixon listening to that missing conversation. Even if it did not, the June 4 tape would reveal which conversations Nixon himself was most concerned about. As such, it might serve as a virtual Rosetta stone unlocking the whole case. At a minimum, the tape would give the special prosecutor a powerful argument down the road: the president himself had determined these twelve hours of conversations with Dean to be relevant. Why else would he waste valuable time listening to them?[12]

Nixon's lawyers were adamantly opposed to giving Jaworski the tape. They saw what the special prosecutor was up to. They also knew things Jaworski did not. The tape captured Nixon and Haig "plotting to ambush" John Dean. It also captured Nixon admitting that he might be personally implicated in the Watergate cover-up. To voluntarily turn over this tape would be like handing Jaworski a loaded gun and hoping he did not know how to use it. Fred

Buzhardt, the cagey Mississippian who replaced Dean as White House counsel, doubted that any special prosecutor could be so inept. He strongly advised Nixon against turning over the tape.[13]

Alexander Haig saw things differently. A former vice chief of staff for the Army and a veteran administrator, Haig was normally an extremely savvy operator. On this occasion, however, the bait in Jaworski's trap was too enticing to resist. Whatever the risks, Haig could not pass up a chance to decisively dispel the black cloud that Watergate had cast over the administration. It seemed too good to be true because it was. But Haig allowed himself to get caught up in the moment. He had firmly convinced himself of Nixon's innocence. If they had nothing to hide, why not prove it by turning over this one tape? Nixon agreed.[14]

On January 8, Jaworski spent much of the day at the White House, listening to the June 4 tape and taking copious notes. The quality of the recording was terrible, however. Could he take a copy with him? This had been a red line for Nixon, and Fred Buzhardt, who was supervising the listening session, categorically refused. Haig overruled him, however, and Jaworski got his copy. A day later, the special prosecutor sent a letter to the White House. He wanted twenty-five more tapes. Haig felt betrayed. Nixon was apoplectic. He had played nice long enough. There would be no more. He would not turn over another tape, ever.[15]

Final Gambits

Leon Jaworski was unbowed. On March 12, he sent another letter to the White House, repeating his prior request and asking for additional tapes. The total was now forty-four. The president was simultaneously considering requests from the House Judiciary Committee, which would vote on impeachment. After a prolonged delay, James St. Clair told Jaworski he would get exactly what the

House Committee got and nothing more. The president was in no rush, either. On April 11, the Committee finally tired of waiting and issued a formal subpoena for forty-four of Nixon's taped conversations. The vote was thirty-three to three.[16]

On April 16, the special prosecutor asked Judge Sirica to issue a subpoena to the president for sixty-four tapes. Because the grand jury had already been dismissed, this would be a "trial subpoena," issued by the court on behalf of the prosecution. As a result, the tapes sought would have to be usable as evidence at trial, which was not true of a grand jury subpoena. This would become crucial later on.[17]

Sirica promptly issued the subpoena, directing the president to deliver the tapes to the court by May 2. Eventually, Nixon would file a motion to quash this subpoena. But first, the president and the special prosecutor each had a final card to play in the high-stakes poker match of public opinion.[18]

Initially, Nixon wanted to defy both the congressional and judicial subpoenas outright, but his lawyers were appalled at this idea. It would make the president look guilty. "We cannot stand the charge of concealment," James St. Clair advised. Fred Buzhardt agreed. They had to throw Congress and the special prosecutor a bone—and it had to be a meaty one.

Yet they also needed to stand their ground on executive privilege. This meant that the president's compliance would have to be presented as voluntary. Just as important, it would have to stake out a reasonable middle ground. This would give Nixon's congressional supporters crucial cover with the public. Otherwise, he "would leave himself open to unending demands for new evidence." The ultimate goal was not legal but political: to make Nixon look well-meaning and reasonable while painting his persecutors in Congress and the special prosecutor's office as rabid extremists.[19] Reluctantly, Nixon acceded.

On April 29, the president delivered his third major speech on Watergate to a nationally televised audience. He sat at a wooden desk before a blue satin curtain. On his right stood a large American flag. On his left was the flag of the president. Judge Sirica's deadline for turning over the subpoenaed tapes was just two days away.

Nixon read deliberately and somewhat haltingly from a sheaf of typewritten pages. He began with a brief and self-serving explanation of the Watergate scandal. Then, he made his dramatic announcement: the next morning he would publicly release edited transcripts of all the tapes requested by the House Judiciary Committee. These transcripts would include only material relevant to the Watergate investigation, as judged by Nixon and his aides. "But everything that is relevant is included—the rough as well as the smooth."

Nixon emphasized that he had not guarded the privacy of the White House tapes to hide his guilt, as many assumed. He had done it to defend the sacred "constitutional doctrine of executive privilege." Now, he was prepared to make an "unprecedented exception" to this privilege. He hoped that doing so would spare the nation from enduring "the wrenching ordeal" of impeachment unnecessarily.

To dramatize the extent of his concession, he directed the attention of the audience to twenty-fix gold-embossed binders stacked next to him. These, he said, were the transcripts that would be released the next day. In reality, the binders were merely a prop. Some of them contained only a single sheet of paper, but that was not discernible on television. "Once and for all," Nixon declared, these transcripts would "show that what I knew and what I did were just as I have described them to you from the very beginning."[20]

Initial reactions to the speech were just what Nixon and his team had hoped. The most important goal had been to shore up Republican congressional support. If Nixon could accomplish that, calls for impeachment would look like garden-variety Democratic partisanship. Key Republican leaders seemed pleased. Senator Barry Goldwater, an important barometer of party opinion, described the president's proposal as "fair and reasonable." Senate minority leader Hugh Scott said the "wealth of material" Nixon promised was proof of "good faith." Illinois representative Robert McClory of the House Judiciary Committee was dryly matter-of-fact. The transcripts, he said, were "both an adequate compliance with the committee's subpoena and sufficient for the committee's investigation." As expected, congressional Democrats voiced far more skepticism, but the White House could live with that. Partisan Democratic opposition was actually part of the plan.[21]

What followed the next day was definitely not part of the plan. A carload of transcripts was delivered to the Capitol in the morning. Meanwhile, the White House press office deliberately delayed public release of the transcripts until late afternoon. This, it was hoped, would force evening news broadcasts to rely on James St. Clair's highly selective summary instead of the transcripts themselves. The president would thus get to frame the public narrative before reporters got their hands on the incriminating details of the transcripts. It was not to be. That night's headlines were full of damning presidential statements from Nixon's March 21 conversation with John Dean: "You have no choice but to come up with the $120,000"; "Keep the cap on the bottle"; "Buy time." Over the next several weeks, the transcripts continued to dominate the headlines. Radio and television programs staged dramatic reenactments. Paperback book editions were rushed into print and sold millions of copies.[22]

Nixon had personally expurgated many of the most incriminating details. Some pages he slashed through completely with red pen. Others he simply threw in the wastebasket. As a result, the published transcripts were deeply misleading in crucial respects.

But it did not much matter. The tone of the conversations was so unsavory, mean-spirited, and just plain shabby that the transcripts destroyed the last shreds of his credibility.

It did not help that Nixon had assiduously cultivated a reputation for moral rectitude. In campaign appearances, he frequently criticized his political opponents for coarsening the nation's public life and demeaning the dignity of high government office. Now the public had seen the real, private Nixon, thinly veiled behind a profusion of "expletive deleted" notations. The contrast with his public persona was stark and devastating. Upon reading the transcripts, White House aide David Gergen remarked in despair: "the President's moral authority is collapsing." In truth, it had already collapsed. But the chances of Nixon ever regaining it seemed slimmer than ever.[23]

During the public uproar over the transcripts, James St. Clair filed his motion to quash the special prosecutor's subpoena. Besides claiming executive privilege as a shield, the motion advanced two new arguments. First, St. Clair claimed that the special prosecutor was part of the executive branch and could not therefore initiate legal action against the president. To do so would violate article III of the Constitution, which limits the jurisdiction of federal courts to "actual cases and controversies." There could be no case or controversy, St. Clair argued, between the executive branch and itself. Second, and most forcefully, he pointed out that evidence sought by a trial subpoena must be admissible under the Federal Rules of Evidence. Since the president himself was not under indictment, the statements on the subpoenaed tapes would be inadmissible hearsay. That, St. Clair argued, made the subpoena invalid.[24]

Unwittingly, St. Clair had forced the special prosecutor's hand. Two months earlier, the grand jury had secretly named Richard Nixon as an unindicted coconspirator. Nixon's out-of-court statements were therefore admissible against his fellow Watergate conspirators under the coconspirator exception to the hearsay rules. This provided Jaworski with a knockdown response to St. Clair's most forceful argument. That was bad enough for president, but it was only the beginning. If the special prosecutor made this argument in court, it would immediately become public. That meant the American people would soon learn that a grand jury had found probable cause to accuse the president of a crime. This gave Jaworski leverage, and he intended to use it.[25]

At 3:30 p.m. on Sunday, May 5, a tan government sedan pulled up to a secluded back entrance to the White House. It carried Leon Jaworski, Philip Lacovara, and Richard Ben-Veniste. Inside the Map Room, next to the Oval Office, Haig was expecting them. St. Clair arrived late, looking puffy and tired. His flight from Boston had been delayed.

When they were all seated, Ben-Veniste passed a transcript of the grand jury's February 25 proceedings to the president's lawyer. Misreading the document, St. Clair grew intensely agitated. He at first thought that the grand jury had secretly *indicted* Nixon. Ben-Veniste corrected him, but St. Clair was hardly mollified. "This is an attempt to embarrass the president," he snapped.[26]

After a brief, tense exchange, Jaworski raised the prospect of compromise. In exchange for a reduced number of tapes, he would drop the subpoena and keep the grand jury's action secret. It would probably come out at trial, but that was several months away at least. With the House impeachment inquiry gearing up, the president had a strong interest in keeping this matter under wraps as long as possible. If the grand jury's action were revealed now, the impact on public opinion might be calamitous. Haig asked for time to think it over. Jaworski agreed, and the meeting adjourned.

On May 7, St. Clair rejected the proposed compromise. Three days later, the special prosecutor filed a brief revealing that the grand jury had named Nixon an unindicted coconspirator. On May

20, Judge Sirica issued a brief opinion denying the president's motion to quash. There was little point in writing at elaborate length. The Supreme Court would obviously have the final word.[27]

"Give 'Em Hell, Leon Baby!"

At 10:02 a.m. on July 8, the eight black-robed justices of the Supreme Court filed into the marble-columned courtroom. One by one, they took their seats behind the raised and slightly bowed mahogany bench. In the center sat the snowy-haired and sanctimonious Warren Burger, looking every inch a chief justice. Nixon had appointed Burger just five years earlier to replace the great liberal lion Earl Warren. Nixon had also appointed Burger's fellow Minnesotan Harry Blackmun and Lewis Powell, the former president of the American Bar Association. As the most junior justices, Blackmun and Powell occupied the outer wings of the bench, farthest from the chief. Thurgood Marshall, the Court's first and only African-American justice, sat three chairs to Burger's right.[28] There were no female justices.

Three lawyers sat facing the justices from behind mahogany counsel tables. James St. Clair appeared on behalf of the president. Leon Jaworski and Philip Lacovara represented the special prosecutor's office. Behind the lawyers, several rows of chairs were arranged for members of the Supreme Court bar and other specially invited guests. A brass railing separated this reserved seating area from the public gallery. Behind the railing, silent, sleepy spectators packed the long pews. Most of them had waited all night for their seats. During the argument, nearly a thousand additional spectators would be permitted to view the proceedings in five minutes shifts.[29]

Without fanfare or acknowledgment of the extraordinary circumstances, Chief Justice Burger drily announced the case. He then turned to the special prosecutor. "You may proceed whenever you are ready, Mr. Jaworski."[30]

Jaworski began with the customary shibboleth: "Mr. Chief Justice and may it please the Court." He then described the history of the case in some detail. He placed particular emphasis on the grand jury's unanimous vote to name Richard Nixon as an unindicted coconspirator. He also stressed the importance of the White House tapes as evidence in the cover-up prosecution of the president's top aides. Quite unusually, the justices allowed Jaworski to speak for more than five minutes without interruption.[31]

After a flurry of questions about the significance of the grand jury's action, the special prosecutor cut to the chase. "This case really presents one fundamental issue," he said. "Who is to be the arbiter of what the Constitution says?" The president's position was that he alone should determine the boundaries of executive privilege. "Now, the president may be right in how he reads the Constitution," Jaworski acknowledged. "But, he may also be wrong. And if he is wrong, who is there to tell him so? And if there's no one, then the President, of course, is free to pursue his course of erroneous interpretations. What then becomes of our constitutional form of government?"[32]

Having made his key point, Jaworski turned to Nixon's jurisdictional objections. In a nutshell, the president's argument was that any litigation between himself and the special prosecutor was an "action between friends." Historically, federal courts have refused to entertain such actions because the Constitution limits the judicial power to situations where the parties have genuinely adverse interests. For this reason, no court would entertain a dispute between the president and the secretary of state or Army chief of staff. A dispute between the president and a special prosecutor, Nixon contended, was no different.[33]

Jaworski offered two distinct arguments in rebuttal. First, he pointed to the regulations authorizing his appointment, which granted him a wide measure of independence from the president. "One of the expressed duties that's delegated to the Special Prosecutor," Jaworski explained, "is that he shall have full authority for investigating and prosecuting allegations involving the President. And a delegation of authority expressly states, in particular: the Special Prosecutor shall have full authority to determine whether or not to contest the assertion of executive privilege." This independence, Jaworski reminded the justices, was "but an echo of public demand."[34]

Second, Jaworski emphasized that the president and the attorney general had repeatedly promised Congress that he would have independent authority to take the president to court. They had specifically promised that Jaworski would have the power to contest the president's assertion of executive privilege. These promises, Jaworski said, were offered to assure Congress that a statutory special prosecutor was unnecessary. Having succeeded in this aim, the president was now trying to go back on this word.[35]

After a few more desultory exchanges on executive privilege, Jaworski reserved the balance of his time for rebuttal. All in all, his performance was halting, hesitant, and somewhat meandering. But the questions he faced were largely friendly, and he managed to make most of the points he needed to. He seemed relieved to relinquish the podium.[36]

The Over Confident Mr. St. Clair

James St. Clair stepped to the podium with a far more relaxed and self-confident manner than Jaworski. His posture, his voice, and his facial expression all communicated a conviction that this was his moment to shine. "Mr. Chief Justice, and members of the Court," he began, slightly flubbing the customary opening. Quickly, he turned to what the case "really involved." That, he said, was a "realistic fusion" of the special prosecutor's investigation and the impeachment proceedings pending in the House of Representatives. Plainly, St. Clair was trying to set up an argument that impeachment was the only constitutional mechanism for holding the president accountable.[37]

Almost immediately, however, he found himself impaled on several technicalities of Supreme Court procedure. At one point, he asked the justices to dispose of the case in a way that would have left Judge Sirica's decision in place. This triggered laughter from those members of the audience who were sufficiently awake and legally sophisticated to appreciate his faux pas. "If we dismiss as improvidently granted," Justice Marshall remarked drily, "I submit the District Court's judgment would stand."

Several other justices pounced on St. Clair's mistakes in quick succession. They seemed almost to take pleasure in raking him over the coals. It was not an auspicious beginning, but St. Clair seemed unperturbed.[38]

When he finally overcame his procedural missteps, the justices continued to pummel him with hostile questions. It was several minutes before he got out his first complete thought: the Court should refuse to decide the case. Deciding it, he said, would "inexorably" mire the Court in the political process of impeachment, which the Constitution allocated solely to Congress. Exactly how a judicial subpoena would interfere with the impeachment process St. Clair could not adequately explain. Nor could he explain how far clear of the impeachment process his argument would require the Court to steer. He could not even explain what it would mean for the Court to refuse to decide a case involving a judicial subpoena. What he wanted, evidently, was not for the Supreme Court to avoid a decision. Rather, he wanted it to decide the case and quash Judge Sirica's subpoena. The justices would have none of it.[39]

Stymied on this front, St. Clair turned to the jurisdictional question. Here, too, skeptical questions nearly prevented him from getting out a complete thought. When he finally did so, his argument took the form of a syllogism: the government of the United States has only three branches—legislative, executive, and judicial. The special prosecutor was unquestionably not a member of the legislative or judicial branch. Therefore, by process of elimination, he must be part of the executive branch. The same branch of government, however, could not be on both sides of a dispute. That was not a true case or controversy of the sort that the Constitution entrusts the courts to decide. Again, this argument seemed to get him nowhere.

Finally, St. Clair moved on to his core argument on executive privilege. Right from the outset, he disastrously conflated that privilege with a distinct legal principle known as the "political question doctrine." Executive privilege protects the privacy of presidential communications. The political question doctrine prohibits courts from deciding questions that the Constitution specifically entrusts to another branch of government. Which was St. Clair trying to argue? The justices wanted to know.

St. Clair could only respond, feebly, that his argument drew on elements of both. After this embarrassment, he never gained any meaningful traction with the Court. The remainder of his time was largely squandered jumping from one peripheral point to another. Along the way, he mentioned the importance of confidential advice to the president. He also mentioned the need for some form of executive privilege to ensure the president would receive candid counsel. Too often, though, he found himself knocked off course or backed into taking unnecessarily extreme positions.[40]

At one point, just as St. Clair seemed to be making some headway, Justice Powell interrupted him with a question: "What public interest is there in preserving secrecy with respect to a criminal conspiracy?" St. Clair responded with a line that might have come from *Alice in Wonderland* or *Catch-22*. "The answer, sir, is that criminal conspiracy is criminal only after it's proven to be criminal." In other words, the special prosecutor could have the evidence needed to prove his criminal charges only if he first proved the charges the evidence was being sought to prove.[41]

Pressed on this point, St. Clair said that the proper remedy was impeachment. Justice Marshall was incredulous: "if you know the President is doing something wrong, you can impeach him, but the only way you can find out is this way. You can't impeach him, so you don't impeach him. You lose me someplace along there!" With that, the first Supreme Court argument of James St. Clair's career sputtered to a conclusion. He did not seem to recognize that it had been an unmitigated disaster.[42]

The Talented Mr. Lacovara

Philip Lacovara rose to the podium wearing the long-tailed morning coat that Leon Jaworski refused to wear because it made him look like a penguin. If anything, the coat probably looked sillier on the short, somewhat schlubby Lacovara than it would have on Jaworski. But there was nothing silly or awkward about the brilliant young lawyer once he opened his mouth. "Thank you, Mr. Chief Justice," Lacovara began. The presentation that followed was a marvel of clarity, precision, and economy. In less than half the time allotted to his elders, Lacovara said at least as much of substance, and he said it far better.[43]

The justices were palpably relieved to have a competent interlocutor before them, and their questions grew crisper and clearer along with Lacovara's answers. He began by deftly cutting through a thorny procedural thicket that had nearly derailed Jaworski. Then, he precisely and persuasively explained why the subpoenaed tapes were relevant to the prosecution of Nixon's top aides. When Lacovara had just a few minutes remaining, Justice William Brennan interrupted. Could he address St. Clair's argument that the subpoena should be quashed out of deference to congressional impeachment proceedings? That, Lacovara said confidently, was just where he was heading.[44]

He proceeded to demolish the president's position. The present dispute, he explained, was nothing like the so-called political questions that the Supreme Court had refused to decide in other cases. It did not involve a jurisdictional dispute between two congressional committees or a dispute between a the president and his cabinet. It was a criminal proceeding in a federal court against six defendants accused of violating the laws of the United States. Nothing could be closer to the heart of the judiciary's constitutional responsibilities.[45]

The Supreme Court's decision would obviously have significant political implications, but that was par for the course. Warming to his point, Lacovara concluded: "perhaps the finest chapter in the Court's recent history has come in the fields of reapportionment, civil rights, and the procedural rights of the criminally accused. It would be naive to say that those were not profoundly politically important decisions, but they were made as decisions of constitutional law despite the consequences that political branches might face. Despite the public reaction, the court understood its duty to interpret the constitution. That's all we ask for today."[46]

The Shadow of the Law

The Supreme Court announced its decision to a packed courtroom at 11 a.m. on July 24. It was unanimous—"eight-zip," as the word spread quickly through the White House corridors. The Court recognized that the Constitution granted the president a limited executive privilege. But the justices concluded that the president's "generalized interest in confidentiality" could not overcome "the specific need for evidence in a pending criminal trial." The Court therefore denied the president's motion to quash the subpoena and ordered him to turn over all sixty-four tapes sought by the special prosecutor. To make matters more painful, Nixon's own appointee, Chief Justice Burger, had written the opinion. St. Clair was shocked. Right up until the announcement, he thought he had won.[47]

The Court's decision was a clear and resounding defeat for the president. It left no room for further maneuvering. Nixon had only two choices. He could defy the Supreme Court, provoking a full-blown constitutional crisis. Alternatively, he could turn over the tapes, which he knew contained the proverbial "smoking gun." On June 23, 1972, less than a week after the Watergate burglary, Nixon had discussed the cover-up with his chief of staff, Bob Haldeman. At that meeting, he ordered Haldeman to get the CIA to squelch the FBI's investigation, citing phony national security concerns. Ironically, Nixon could probably have avoided releasing this tape if he had been willing to compromise earlier. It was one of the last to make the special prosecutor's list of sixty-four. Jaworski might well have bargained it away in a negotiated settlement.[48]

Both paths were nearly certain to end in impeachment and removal from office. Outraged by the Court's decision and the betrayal by his own appointees, Nixon dithered for most of the day. Late that evening, he grudgingly directed his press secretary Ron Ziegler to make a public statement: the president would comply with the Court's decision "in all respects." For two more weeks, he twisted agonizingly in the wind, as revelations from the tapes cost him his last remaining support in Congress. Finally, Richard

M. Nixon accepted the inevitable and resigned the presidency, effective at noon on August 8, 1974.[49]

As the immediate catalyst for Nixon's resignation, the Supreme Court's decision in *United States v. Nixon* was enormously significant in its own right. It has also cast a long shadow over subsequent executive privilege disputes. Most of these disputes, however, have been resolved through negotiation outside of court. Partly that is because the *Nixon* decision is so vague that neither side can be confident about how any future case might come out. Partly it is because the considerations at stake are so sensitive. As a result, neither special prosecutors nor presidents have been eager to press their position to the hilt.

Special prosecutors worry about establishing bad judicial precedents, limiting their access to presidential testimony and documentary evidence. They also worry about appearing like overzealous partisans, being fired, or provoking the president to outright defiance of a judicial order. Presidents worry about appearing guilty or lawless. Why would a president refuse to testify or turn over evidence unless he had something to hide?[50]

The upshot is that both sides have a strong interest in compromise. Historically, this is how most executive privilege disputes have been resolved. Presidents Bill Clinton, George H. W. Bush, and Ronald Reagan all testified as part of special prosecutor investigations under terms negotiated by their lawyers. In each case, those terms gave special prosecutors less than they might have obtained in court but at lower legal and political risk.

If special prosecutors had decided to subpoena these presidents, the *Nixon* decision would have given them a powerful legal argument. That argument is made even stronger by the Supreme Court's 1996 decision permitting Paula Jones to proceed with her civil suit against a sitting president. One ordinary incident of a civil case is compulsory deposition under oath by lawyers of the opposing side. If a president must submit to this burden in a mere civil case, why should the same rule not apply to criminal cases? The public interest at stake in the latter is considerably higher.[51]

Yet these arguments are far from ironclad. For one thing, a request for live presidential testimony is unquestionably more intrusive than the request for recordings that the Supreme Court upheld in *United States v. Nixon*. To testify under oath, a president must be present for questioning and, realistically, must also spend substantial time preparing to testify. The review and production of recordings or documents can be outsourced to the president's lawyers. The duty of testifying under oath cannot. For this reason, some influential historical sources support the existence of a presidential privilege against compelled testimony. These include Thomas Jefferson and the great early Supreme Court justice Joseph Story. If the courts could command the president, Jefferson reasoned, they "could bandy him from pillar to post and withdraw him entirely from his constitutional duties."[52]

In the Paula Jones case, the Supreme Court rejected similar arguments about the risks of subjecting presidents to civil suit. But the Court has never explicitly addressed the question of presidential testimony. The power of a court to compel the president to testify under oath, therefore, remains an open question. The scope of executive privilege over documents and records is somewhat clearer because the Supreme Court directly addressed it in *United States v. Nixon*. But the rule established in that case depends on a hazy judicial balancing of interests. That makes going to court risky for both sides.[53]

The biggest risk, for both special prosecutors and presidents, is political rather than legal. A president who refuses a reasonable request for documents or testimony looks like he has something to hide. The last president who outright refused such a request was Richard Nixon, and he really did have something to hide. This lesson of Watergate remains deeply ingrained in American political consciousness. Special prosecutors, too, have powerful reasons to consider public opinion. At any time, they might be fired by the president whose administration they are investigating. If special prosecutors push too hard or appear heedless of the president's status as a democratically elected leader, that will only make it easier to justify shutting down their investigations.[54]

The relative strength of these countervailing pressures varies from case to case. Mostly the balance turns on the public's assessment of the president's culpability and confidence in the impartiality and good judgment of the special prosecutor. But in general, these factors have favored compromise. That is why presidents Clinton, Bush, and Reagan all voluntarily agreed, in quite varied circumstances, to testify under oath.[55] Even Watergate illustrates the powerful pressure on both sides to compromise. As late as April 1974, Richard Nixon still hoped the American people would accept his edited transcripts as a sensible middle ground. Earlier that year, Leon Jaworski and Alexander Haig engaged in substantial and fruitful negotiations. Had Nixon been less paranoid and more coolly rational, some compromise might well have been reached.

Together, these historical precedents create a powerful gravitational pull toward compromise going forward. A future president who refuses to do what prior presidents have done will look unreasonable—and guilty—by comparison. The same goes for special prosecutors, except that they risk appearing overzealous rather than guilty. Still, the weight of history is only one of several factors that enter into the calculus. If a president has succeeded in discrediting a special prosecutor with the public he may be emboldened to refuse any cooperation. If the shoe is on the other foot, a special prosecutor might feel confident enough to push for a decisive resolution in court.

The matter is further complicated by an ambiguous 1988 memorandum issued by the Office of Legal Counsel. According to this memo, sitting presidents may be subpoenaed to testify but "are not required to testify in person at criminal trials." The implication is that presidents are too busy to be ordered by a court to testify at any particular place, date, and time. They can, however, be required to testify through alternative arrangements that adequately accommodate the many other pressing demands of the presidency. What those alternative arrangements might be in any particular case is unclear. But the voluntary arrangements struck by previous presidents provide suggestive examples that a court might seek to follow. This memo is probably binding on special counsels under current Justice Department regulations. Its ambiguity adds another layer of uncertainty to an already hazy legal question. This uncertainty gives both sides another reason to compromise.[56]

Ultimately, the overarching question remains: What will the American people tolerate? Here, too, the choice is ours.

8

Can the President Obstruct Justice?

At least since Watergate, political wags have smugly asserted: "it's not the crime. It's the cover-up." Like most well-worn catchphrases, this one is silly and glib if taken literally. But it also contains an important kernel of truth. A surprising number of presidential scandals have involved alleged attempts to cover up wrongdoing, often by the president's subordinates rather than the president. To take the most obvious example, the first article of impeachment against Richard Nixon was "obstruction of justice." The second was "abuse of power." Both were based on overlapping allegations that Nixon had impaired "the due and proper administration of justice and the conduct of lawful inquiries."[1]

Other examples abound. The Iran-Contra scandal turned heavily on allegations that senior Reagan administration officials covered up the funneling of money and arms to Nicaraguan rebels. Ronald Reagan was never directly implicated in this cover-up. But there is reason to believe that his vice president, George H. W. Bush, might have been, had the investigation been allowed to proceed.[2]

Bill Clinton was impeached solely based on his attempt to cover up an extramarital affair with White House intern Monica Lewinsky. The articles of impeachment against him included perjury before a federal grand jury, obstruction of justice, and abuse of power. Ultimately, Clinton was acquitted of all charges in the Senate. Still, only two other presidents in history have come so close to being removed from office. The sole basis for this monumental undertaking was an alleged cover-up.[3]

Finally, the possibility of an illegal cover-up was central to special counsel Robert Mueller's investigation. Mueller seriously investigated whether Trump obstructed justice by asking FBI director James Comey to back off the investigation of national security advisor Michael Flynn. Mueller also investigated whether Trump fired Comey to interfere with the FBI's Russia investigation. Finally, Mueller investigated whether Trump attempted to harass attorney general Jeff Sessions into resigning in order to obstruct Mueller's investigation.[4]

In light of this history, it might appear strange to ask: "Can the president obstruct justice?" The answer would seem obviously to be yes. That is probably correct, but the issue is more complicated than it initially appears. The Constitution makes the president the nation's chief law enforcement officer. For this reason, several prominent lawyers and legal scholars have argued that a president cannot unlawfully interfere with a federal investigation. After all, the Constitution empowers the president, and the president alone, to "take care that the laws shall be faithfully executed."[5]

In plain English, the president is the boss of the whole federal law enforcement apparatus, including the FBI and the Justice Department. If he decides that the FBI director should be fired for pursuing an espionage investigation too aggressively, that is the president's decision to make. Put differently, the president cannot obstruct justice because the president decides what justice consists of, so far as federal law enforcement is concerned. The idea is well captured by Richard Nixon's famous—and notorious—plea in self-defense: "when the President does it, that means it is not illegal."[6]

Critics of this argument respond that the president's powers as chief executive are subject to legal limits. Just as the president could not lawfully accept a bribe to drop criminal charges, he cannot interfere with a federal investigation to protect himself or his friends. To do so would be to act for a "corrupt purpose," which is the hallmark of obstruction of justice. Nothing in the constitutional powers of the president permits him to misuse his office in this way. This argument is supported by recent historical practice, which strongly suggests that the president can commit the crime of obstruction of justice and that this crime can rise to the level of an impeachable offense.[7] Still, no court has ever formally decided this question, and it remains the subject of discussion and debate.

The Anatomy of Obstruction

Lawyers define crimes by their essential elements: the precise facts that a prosecutor must prove to convict a person of the crime. There are several federal obstruction of justice statutes, which establish subtly different crimes, but all share the same three core elements. The first element goes by the hoary Latin name "actus reus," or "guilty act." This means an act that "influences, obstructs, or impedes"—or *attempts* to influence, obstruct, or impede—the due administration of justice. The second element is a "corrupt" or improper purpose. This is also called the "mens rea," or "guilty mind," requirement. The third element is an ongoing or future federal "proceeding" that the accused individual seeks to obstruct.[8]

Each element can be tricky in its own way. The guilty act element, for instance, requires an affirmative act, not a mere omission. The destruction of evidence or threatening of a grand jury witness surely qualifies. A passive failure to assist federal law enforcement is not sufficient. This explains why President Reagan was never formally accused of obstructing the investigation into the Iran-Contra affair. Reagan seems to have known about his subordinates' efforts to impede a congressional investigation. But a seven-year independent counsel investigation never turned up hard evidence that Reagan himself actively authorized, instigated, or orchestrated these efforts.[9]

In this way, the guilty act element narrows the range of conduct that qualifies as obstruction of justice. In other respects, however, that element sweeps quite broadly. An effort to influence, obstruct, or impede the due administration of justice need not succeed in order to qualify as a crime. Conduct that merely attempts or "endeavors to" obstruct justice is enough. If oil baron Edward Doheny bribed Albert Fall to lie before the grand jury, that would constitute a guilty act even if Fall told the whole truth. Nor is it necessary that there be an underlying crime to conceal. Bribing Fall to lie would still constitute a guilty act even if the oil lease he awarded Doheny violated no law. As legal scholars Daniel Hemel and Eric Posner put it, "obstruction of justice is an independent crime."[10]

This sometimes leads critics to dismiss obstruction of justice as a manufactured offense of no real significance—the last refuge of desperate, partisan prosecutors. Stated so baldly, this argument cannot withstand scrutiny. The investigation of crimes is an indispensable function of government. The deliberate obstruction of that function, even by a defendant innocent of any underlying crime, threatens the integrity of the legal system. In effect, such conduct amounts to an assertion that the defendant is entitled to control his—or her—own investigation and prosecution. No legal system can afford to let such effrontery go systematically unpunished.[11]

The severity of obstruction of justice, however, falls along a spectrum. A civil defendant who lies about a peripheral matter in a deposition has probably violated one or more federal obstruction of justice statutes. But such conduct would rarely be prosecuted in ordinary circumstances. The same goes for many technical instances of obstruction in criminal cases charging minor crimes or involving minor efforts to influence a federal proceeding. On the other hand, the flagrant and sustained abuse of official power to obstruct the investigation of serious crimes is a very grave offense. This is true even if the crimes under investigation cannot be proven or were never committed. Unfortunately, the obstruction of justice statutes do not themselves draw these distinctions. A judicious prosecutor must therefore exercise prudence and restraint in deciding whether to bring charges for obstruction of justice.[12]

So much for the guilty act element. What about corrupt or improper purpose? For most individuals charged with obstruction of justice, this is the easiest and most straightforward element of the crime. That is because most people have no plausibly legitimate business influencing, obstructing, or impeding the administration of justice. Any ordinary person who intentionally interferes with a federal investigation or judicial proceeding is probably motivated by an improper purpose. No precise definition of propriety is required to know that a defendant who intimidates a juror is behaving improperly. The same goes for the friend or lover or criminal associate of a defendant who engages in the same conduct. It does not matter if the defendant is innocent of the underlying crime or sincerely afraid of being framed by the police. Any intentional attempt to interfere with a judicial proceeding by an ordinary citizen is ipso facto—"by that very fact"—the product of an improper purpose.[13]

Other persons, however, have perfectly lawful reasons for seeking to influence—or even impede—the administration of justice. Edward Doheny's lawyer gave a masterful, tear-jerking closing argument that resulted in the acquittal of his client for bribery. But no one would say he had obstructed justice. No one would say this even if Doheny's attorney knew that his client was guilty, as he probably did. In the context of America's adversary system of justice, there is nothing improper about a defense attorney seeking the acquittal of a guilty client.[14]

Similarly, if the Teapot Dome special prosecutors determined that Doheny was too feeble to stand trial after the murder of his son, people might have questioned their judgment. But no one would have accused them of committing a federal crime. In a literal sense, their decision to drop the charges against Doheny would have impeded his prosecution. But under the circumstances, their purpose in making that decision would have been entirely proper. It is a prosecutor's job to make exactly this sort of prudential judgment about which cases ultimately merit prosecution.[15]

This does not mean that a prosecutor can never obstruct justice. If the special prosecutors had scuttled the case against Doheny in exchange for a bribe, they would obviously have acted from an improper purpose and would be guilty of obstruction of justice. The very same action, in other words, can be perfectly legal when undertaken for a legitimate purpose and a federal crime when undertaken for an illegitimate one.[16]

The broad discretion of prosecutors to make charging decisions would be no defense. In 2016, the attorney general of Pennsylvania, Kathleen Kane, was convicted of obstruction of justice under state law. Prosecutors alleged that Kane had directed her subordinates not to investigate illegal leaks that she herself was responsible for. A jury convicted. There are many legitimate reasons why an attorney general, the state's top prosecutor, might move to shut down an investigation. But concealing her own criminal conduct is not among them.[17]

The same basic principles apply to the president. As the nation's chief executive, the president has both the authority and the responsibility to make decisions about federal law enforcement, including criminal prosecutions. Often, those decisions will have the literal effect of impeding or obstructing the federal investigation and prosecution of crimes. In most cases, however, the president's purpose for acting will be obviously proper for a person with his responsibilities. When President Barack Obama directed U.S. attorneys to place a low priority on marijuana prosecutions in states that have legalized the drug, critics questioned his judgment. But no one contended that he had obstructed justice, because his purpose for taking this action was manifestly proper. It is at the core of the president's job to set priorities for the allocation of scarce federal law enforcement resources.[18]

There are even circumstances when a president might legitimately act to influence or impede the prosecution of a particular individual. For example, if a federal prosecutor seeks to subpoena a Canadian diplomat, the president might well intercede to protect the nation's foreign relations. That is just what Ronald Reagan's State Department did when this actually happened in 1982. So, too, a new president might properly direct federal prosecutors not to pursue charges against members of the outgoing administration. Such a directive might be intended to promote national unity or simply to avoid the appearance of criminalizing political differences. This is the course Barack Obama followed when he faced pressure to prosecute senior Bush administration officials for torture.

Absent strong evidence of ulterior motive, no one in either of these cases could plausibly accuse the president of obstructing justice.[19] The main difference between a president and a prosecutor is that the president has a far broader array of responsibilities, including military and foreign affairs. The president can therefore act from a much broader range of proper purposes.

Even the president's authority, however, is subject to limits. If the president ordered federal prosecutors to ignore evidence against his close friend he would clearly be acting with an improper purpose. So, too, if the president ordered an investigation shut down in exchange for a bribe or to protect a politician of his own party. The president is not entrusted with law enforcement authority to protect his friends, to enrich himself, or to rig the political process. If he attempts to influence or impede federal law enforcement in pursuit of these ends he commits obstruction of justice.[20]

These are the clear cases. There are also closer ones. Sometimes it will be difficult to determine the president's motive. Even when that motive can be discerned, it will often be complex, encompassing both legitimate and illegitimate considerations. Finally, the distinction between illegitimate pursuit of partisan advantage and legitimate consideration of public opinion may be fuzzy at the margin. A President does not obstruct justice simply by pursuing policies he believes will make him popular with the public or members of his party. But it will not always be easy to draw the line between permissible conduct of this kind and impermissible abuse of the presidency for partisan advantage.[21]

The existence of difficult cases should not obscure the fundamental point. Some purposes are clearly improper even for a president. They are not necessary for the president to carry out his constitutional responsibilities. To the contrary, they violate his constitutional duty to "take care that the laws shall be faithfully executed." A president who attempts to interfere with federal law enforcement for one of these purposes commits obstruction of justice.[22]

Actually, that is not quite right—or at least it is not quite complete. To obstruct justice in violation of federal law, the actions of the president or anyone else must be directed at a "proceeding." This is the third and final element of the crime of obstruction of justice. The basic idea is that obstruction cannot occur in the abstract. An individual must obstruct, or seek to obstruct, *something*—namely, a concrete government effort to enforce the laws of the United States. Such an effort is called a "proceeding," and different statutes define this term differently. The most restrictive definition is limited to court proceedings, including grand jury proceedings. The broadest encompasses "any proceeding before Congress or a Federal Government agency which is authorized by law." Courts have split on whether this definition includes criminal investigations conducted by the FBI, but it probably does, at least if the investigation is one that "foreseeably leads to a grand jury probe."[23]

Putting it all together, the crime of obstruction of justice consists of obstructing or attempting to obstruct a federal proceeding for an improper purpose. Many complexities lurk in this apparently simple definition, but none affects the bottom line. The president of the United States is fully capable of committing the statutory offense of obstruction of justice. The only question is whether the Constitution grants the president such absolute law enforcement power as to place him effectively above the law. Both history and logic strongly suggest that the answer is no.

The Smoking Gun

On June 23, 1972, just six days after the Watergate burglary, Richard Nixon's chief of staff broached a delicate subject with his boss. Not yet fifty years old and sporting a tight, high crewcut, Bob Haldeman was an intense and self-serious former advertising executive. He first rose to national prominence for his role in orchestrating Nixon's remarkable political renaissance during the 1968 presidential campaign. After losing the 1960 presidential election to John F. Kennedy, Nixon was widely viewed as an embittered has-been, uncharismatic and unsuited to national politics in the age of television. Haldeman, however, astutely recognized the former vice president's potential to tap into the simmering racial and cultural grievances of the late 1960s. He also recognized that Nixon made a far better impression—sunnier, less aggrieved, and more forthright—when he was well-rested. By slashing Nixon's campaign travel and leveraging his own advertising background, Haldeman built an effective and ultimately successful campaign strategy around this insight. No other single person was more instrumental in propelling Richard Nixon to the presidency. Ironically, few would contribute more to his downfall.[24]

"Now, on the investigation," Haldeman said. "You know, the Democratic break-in thing? We are back in the problem area because the FBI is not under control." This was not his first conversation with the president on the subject, and Haldeman jumped right to the grubby details. The investigation, he explained, was "now leading into some productive areas because they've been able to trace the money through the bank, and it goes in some directions we don't want it to go."[25]

The money in question was that paid to the Watergate burglars, which the FBI was on the verge of tracing to Nixon's campaign committee. It did not take a genius to see that this had the makings of a political calamity. As usual, however, Haldeman had a plan. In this case, the plan was actually John Mitchell's idea. After a careful analysis, White House counsel John Dean had also signed off. The plan was simple. The president would order the deputy CIA director to call FBI director Patrick Gray "and just say, 'Stay the hell out of this. This is business we don't want you to go any further on.'" Both Mitchell and Dean agreed with Haldeman that this was the administration's only play.[26]

Nixon was momentarily confused. "What about Pat Gray? You mean he doesn't want to?" He seemed to think that the FBI was refusing to cooperate.

Haldeman patiently explained that the FBI director would need an excuse to call off the investigation. A request from the CIA would give it to him. Coincidentally, several of the Watergate burglars had been recruited from the Cuban exile community in Miami. The Miami Cubans had connections with the CIA dating back to the Bay of Pigs invasion ordered by Nixon's old nemesis, John F. Kennedy. For this reason, Haldeman explained, "we're set up beautifully to do it." Because Cubans were involved, the FBI already suspected that the burglary was a CIA job. The president had only to arrange for the CIA to confirm this erroneous suspicion, and "that would take care of it." The FBI would shut down its investigation before tracing any aspect of the burglary to the Nixon campaign.[27]

The president was still not tracking. Was the plan for his campaign operatives to implicate the CIA? Would they just lie and say that the Cubans had approached them to make the whole thing look like a national security matter? Haldeman acknowledged that this was one possible strategy but quickly pointed out the obvious risk: "then we're relying on more and more people all the time. That's the problem."[28]

"All right. Fine," Nixon said.

"The thing to do is to get them"—the FBI—"to stop."

"Right, fine," the president agreed, finally grasping the point. "How do you do call him in? Well, we protected Helms"—the CIA director—"from one hell of a lot of things." Nixon seemed to think that shutting down an FBI investigation was the least that Richard Helms could do for him in return.[29]

Haldeman agreed.

Nixon wrapped up the conversation by giving Haldeman a script for his call with the CIA. "When you get these people, say: 'Look, this will open the whole Bay of Pigs thing." Nixon trailed off. "Don't lie to them. Just say this is sort of a comedy of errors, bizarre, without getting into it. They should call the FBI in and say that we wish for the country, 'Don't go any further into this case, period!' "[30]

This was a complete fabrication. Nixon was not actually worried about national security or foreign relations. The Cuban émigrés among the Watergate burglars were not actually involved in any active CIA operation. It was all a sham concocted to protect president's closest aides from criminal investigation and Nixon himself from untold political damage. It was also utterly ineffective. By the time Haldeman called deputy CIA director Vernon Walters, the FBI was no longer running the investigation. Earl Silbert's team at the U.S. attorney's office had taken over. The horse was out of the barn.[31]

This episode poses an almost perfect test of the argument that a president cannot obstruct justice. As head of the executive branch, the president unquestionably possesses constitutional authority to supervise the FBI and the CIA. If the Constitution permits him to exercise this authority for any reason, there could be nothing improper about Nixon's actions. Yet when the White House released a transcript of this conversation on August 5, 1974, it almost immediately became known as "the smoking gun." No one quibbled that the president had failed in his effort to shut down the Watergate probe. Nor did anyone contend that the Constitution empowered the president to take this action based on phony national security concerns. Rather, all eleven Republicans who had voted against impeachment on July 30—true Nixon diehards all—announced that they would change their votes. The evidence that the president had committed obstruction of justice was now irrefutably clear, and it cost Nixon his last remaining congressional support. He resigned the presidency three days after releasing the transcript.[32]

"We Were Never Really Alone, Right?"

The day after his deposition in the Paula Jones case, President Bill Clinton called his long-time personal secretary, Betty Currie. As Currie remembered it, Clinton asked her to come to the White House "just to talk about a few things." A diminutive and elegant woman of fifty-eight, Currie was no ordinary secretary. By any fair measure, she was an accomplished and savvy Washington hand. After attending high school in Waukegan, Illinois, she began her secretarial career working for the U.S. Navy. From there, she worked her way up through several federal agencies before becoming secretary to Peace Corps Director Joseph Blatchford in 1969.

Diligent, efficient, shrewd, and highly competent, Currie impressed everyone she worked for. This included her superiors on the 1984, 1988, and 1992 Democratic presidential campaigns. After assisting political strategist James Carville in the Clinton campaign's Little Rock "War Room," she followed Clinton to the White House. She remained in this position for his entire eight-year term.[33]

Currie arrived at the White House at approximately 5 p.m. on Sunday, January 18, 1998. Her elderly mother had been released from the hospital that day, and this was the earliest she could make it. The president began by explaining that he had been formally deposed the previous day in the Paula Jones sexual harassment lawsuit. Currie already knew this, but the next thing Clinton told her came as a shock. Paula Jones's lawyers had asked about White House intern Monica Lewinsky. As Clinton's personal secretary, Currie was the gatekeeper to the Oval Office. She knew who Lewinsky was and when she had been to see the president. She also knew that Lewinsky had "a very serious crush on the President."[34]

A religious, churchgoing woman known for her modesty, Currie prided herself on believing the best about people. She was not naïve or gullible, far from it. But if anything untoward were going on between the president and this young woman, she had not wanted to know. There had certainly been signs, but Currie had deliberately refused to acknowledge them to herself. Now, however, Clinton began to ask her a series of very suspicious leading questions, with the pretense of trying to refresh his own recollections.[35]

When Currie recalled the episode later before Ken Starr's grand jury, she hesitated over the exact wording. But she clearly recalled the gist of Clinton's questions: "you were always there when Monica was there, right? We were never really alone, right? Monica came on to me, and I never touched her, right? She wanted to have sex with me, and I can't do that, right? You could see and hear everything, right?" Currie had not been able to see and hear everything and had no way of knowing what happened outside her direct observation. Nevertheless, she answered in the affirmative.[36]

Two days later, Clinton called Currie after midnight. She was sound asleep, and it took her a minute to understand what he was talking about. He wanted to know if she had seen the news on the internet. The *Drudge Report*, then in its infancy, was running a shocking story: former White House employee Linda Tripp had recorded Monica Lewinsky luridly describing her sexual encounters with the president. Had Currie seen it? She had not. Could she reach Monica? She would try.

The conversation went on for nearly an hour. But when Currie testified about it later, she could not recall what else had been said. At one point, she thought, "Gee, would he please get off the phone because I want to go to bed?" The following day Currie told Clinton that she had not been able to reach Monica. "The only thing I got was this message from her that she couldn't talk to me." The president again walked Currie through the same set of leading questions he had asked her on Sunday. It was January 21, the day the Monica Lewinsky story first broke in the mainstream national media.[37]

These conversations would become the crux of Ken Starr's case that Bill Clinton had committed obstruction of justice. There were various other supporting allegations: Clinton had directly or indirectly supplied Lewinsky with a set of talking points to shut up Linda Tripp. Clinton had asked Vernon Jordan to procure Lewinsky a job in exchange for her silence. Clinton had asked Currie to retrieve and conceal a box of gifts he had given to Lewinsky during their relationship. All of these charges, however, rested on disputed or otherwise problematic evidence. Lewinsky herself repeatedly denied that anyone had ever asked her to lie or promised a job in exchange for her silence. Bill Clinton's apparent efforts to coach Betty Currie were the best and clearest evidence of obstruction that Starr's team turned up.[38]

Both Clinton and Currie would later claim that these conversations were sincere attempts by the president to refresh his recollection. This is almost impossible to believe. Yet, at the times Clinton spoke with Currie, she had not yet been named as a witness in any proceeding. This gave Clinton a colorable argument that he was simply worried about public exposure. Alternatively, and somewhat more plausibly, Clinton may have been trying to figure out which misleading but technically true statements he could get away with. As in any obstruction of justice case, motive was crucial; the evidence of Clinton's was less than ironclad. None of this deterred the House of Representatives, which voted to impeach Bill Clinton for obstruction of justice on December 19, 1998.

This episode sheds important additional light on the debate over whether a president can obstruct justice. At the most basic level, a majority of the House obviously concluded that a president was capable of obstructing justice. This majority included many still prominent Republicans. Many Democrats almost certainly agreed that a president could obstruct justice but voted against impeachment for other reasons.

As a historical precedent, however, this vote is less significant than it initially appears. Bill Clinton was accused of perjury and witness tampering in a civil case. This conduct could not plausibly be characterized as an exercise of his constitutional powers to supervise the executive branch. The president has no constitutional authority to determine whether a civil case goes forward. Even if he had such authority, it would not much help his position. Clinton was not accused of trying to shut down the civil case against him—or the subsequent criminal investigation initiated by the independent counsel. He was accused of corrupting those proceedings by encouraging Betty Currie and others to perjure themselves.

As a purely theoretical exercise, it is possible to construct a partial and strained constitutional defense on Clinton's behalf. The president's greater constitutional power to shut down a federal criminal investigation could conceivably include the lesser power of throwing sand in its gears. But even the most zealous defenders of presidential power do not generally push the point this far. Rather, they distinguish between conduct within the scope of the president's constitutional powers and conduct outside that scope. When the president exercise his authority to supervise and control federal law enforcement, his actions cannot be criminalized by Congress. But when the president acts outside this authority, Congress is free to regulate—and even criminalize—that behavior. Clinton's apparent efforts to influence Currie's testimony pretty clearly fall in the latter category.

This view is narrower and more defensible than a categorical insistence that the president can never obstruct justice. But it would still have perverse and deeply disturbing consequences. For starters, it would permit Congress to criminalize relatively petty forms of obstruction, like Bill Clinton's, while immunizing far more serious abuses of power, like Richard Nixon's. If the Constitution empowers the president to shut down any federal investigation for any reason, Congress is hamstrung. It can do nothing to stop a president from exercising this awesome power in exchange for campaign contributions, political endorsements, or cash bribes. Applying the same theory to the president's other constitutional powers would produce some truly anomalous results. The president could use his authority as commander-in-chief to sell U.S. military aid to the highest bidder, including foreign powers. Perhaps this is the law, but that seems hard to believe.

"Flynn's a Good Guy"

On Valentine's Day of 2016, FBI Director James Comey sat in a semicircle of six chairs facing the presidential desk known as *Resolute*. Built from the oak planks of an Arctic exploration vessel, this desk had been used by twenty-two presidents prior its current occupant, Donald Trump. To conceal his leg braces, Franklin Roosevelt had commissioned an oak frontispiece bearing the presidential seal to cover the kneehole. This modification gave the desk the appearance of a massive, solid block of wood separating the president from his audience.

Besides Comey, that audience included Attorney General Jeff Sessions, Vice-President Mike Pence, and several top intelligence officials. This group was gathered at the White House to brief President Trump on terrorist threats to the United States.[39] The briefing did not take long. To Comey, the president appeared "oddly uninterested and distracted," almost bored. There was little energy or sense of urgency in the room. Though Comey had some disquieting classified information to relay, Trump was impassive. He asked no questions.

When the meeting was over, the president loudly thanked the group, as if relieved to be finished with a dull and unpleasant chore. Then, he pointed at Comey. "I just want to talk to Jim," he said, pointedly. His tone clearly indicated that he wished everyone else to leave. Comey grew nervous. Less than a month into the new president's term, this was the fourth time Trump had sought to meet with him alone. These meetings worried Comey deeply. In place of the FBI's much-cherished independence, he suspected that Trump was seeking to establish "some sort of patronage relationship."[40]

As others filed out of the Oval Office, Jeff Sessions and the president's son-in-law Jared Kushner lingered hesitantly. Both appeared to grasp the impropriety of Trump's request but seemed powerless to do anything about it. The president curtly excused each of them in turn. When the room was clear, Trump turned a blunt gaze on Comey. At six feet eight, the FBI director towered over almost everyone he met, including the six-foot-three Trump. But even to a man of James Comey's formidable stature and long experience, the presidency possesses an awesome majesty. Sitting opposite the president behind his imposing and historic desk, Comey felt as if he were sitting at the foot of a throne.[41]

"I want to talk about Mike Flynn," Trump said flatly.

General Michael Flynn, Trump's first national security advisor and fiery campaign surrogate, had been fired the previous day. His dismissal followed press reports that Flynn had lied about his telephone calls with the Russian ambassador Sergey Kislyak during the presidential transition. Those calls had been picked up by federal wiretaps of Kislyak's phone. As a result, FBI investigators knew that Flynn had asked Kislyak to block a UN resolution condemning Israeli settlements. Flynn had also promised Kislyak that President Trump would repeal the mild sanctions Barack Obama imposed as retaliation for Russian election meddling.[42]

When the press first reported these calls, Vice President Pence publicly insisted that Flynn and Kislyak had merely exchanged pleasantries. He specifically denied that they had discussed U.S. sanctions, explaining that Flynn told him so directly. Later that month, at Comey's direction, FBI investigators had interviewed Flynn at the White House. As a former director of the Defense Intelligence Agency, Flynn should have known that his calls with Kislyak were recorded. All calls of Russian officials in the United States are. Nevertheless, Flynn lied to the investigators, denying that he and Kislyak had discussed either sanctions or the UN resolution.

On January 26, the Justice Department advised the president that Flynn might be susceptible to Russian blackmail over his lies to federal agents. The Russians, after all, knew the truth about the calls. Yet, for more than two weeks, Trump took no action. Only on February 13, when the *New York Times* and *Washington Post* reported that Trump had been warned about Flynn's lies weeks earlier, did the president demand Flynn's resignation.[43]

Trump now explained that decision to Comey. There was nothing wrong with Flynn's calls to Kislyak, he said. In this, he was mostly correct, at least as a legal matter. A 220-year-old federal law called "the Logan Act" prohibits any U.S. citizen from conducting unauthorized negotiations with a foreign power. But no person has ever been convicted of violating it. Regardless, Trump said, Flynn had lied to the vice-president. That meant he had to go.[44]

Agitated by the newspaper reports that had forced his hand on Flynn, Trump launched an extended tirade against leaks to the media. On this subject, he and Comey saw eye to eye, and the FBI director momentarily thought he might have dodged a bullet. Perhaps he could just run out the clock? He explained to Trump how difficult it was to prosecute leakers because doing so generally required the cooperation of recalcitrant media witnesses. This prompted Trump to reminisce fondly about "how we once put reporters in jail and that made them talk."[45]

At this point, the door to the Oval Office opened several inches. White House chief of staff Reince Priebus poked his balding head into view. Trump motioned to Priebus to close the door, which he quickly did. The interruption seemed to remind the president of his original purpose. Mike Flynn, he said to Comey, "is a good guy and has been through a lot." After repeating his earlier explanation for firing Flynn, he added, "I hope you can see your way clear to letting Flynn go. He is a good guy. I hope you can let this go."[46]

Comey was aghast. As he understood Trump's thinly veiled request, the president was asking him to drop the criminal investigation into Flynn's lies. His motive for doing so appeared to be personal regard or sympathy. Comey did not challenge Trump, responding only that Flynn was "a good guy." But he was sufficiently concerned that he immediately prepared a memorandum documenting the conversation. Comey had never felt the need to take this precaution with President Bush or President Obama. This was the second time he had done so with Trump.

The next day, the FBI director pleaded with a shifty-eyed Jeff Sessions never to let it happen again. "You are my boss," he said urgently. "You have to be between me and the president." Sessions simply stared down at his desk. Later, Comey testified before the Senate that he considered Trump's request "an order." He also concluded that Trump must have known he was doing something wrong. Why else would he have "ejected everyone, including my boss and the vice president, from the room so he could speak with me alone?"[47]

Firing the FBI Director

Comey did not shut down the investigation of Michael Flynn. Three months later, he was delivering a routine pep talk at the

FBI's Los Angeles field office. As he spoke, the breaking news chyrons on the wall-mounted televisions behind his audience announced: "Comey Resigns." Confused, he thought it must be an elaborate prank. But quickly some variant of "FBI Director Fired" appeared on three different news networks.

After a flurry of perplexing phone calls, Comey's assistant emailed him a scanned copy of his formal dismissal letter. It said that Attorney General Sessions and Deputy Attorney General Rod Rosenstein had recommended his firing. The ostensible justification was that Comey had violated Justice Department policy by publicly commenting on Hillary Clinton's private email server during the 2016 campaign. This, the letters said, had been unfair to the Democratic presidential candidate. Trump's letter thanked Comey for "informing me on three separate occasions that I am not under investigation" and wished him good luck in his future endeavors.[48]

Public reaction to Comey's dismissal was swift and skeptical. During the 2016 presidential campaign, Trump had repeatedly criticized the FBI for handling Hillary Clinton with kid gloves. Now he was firing the FBI director for being too hard on her? Many Democrats were still irate at Comey's actions during the election, but this did not pass the laugh test. Quickly, Trump added fuel to the fire. In a now famous *NBC News* interview, he explained that he had decided to fire Comey before receiving the attorney general's recommendation. "Regardless of recommendation, I was going to fire Comey," Trump said. "When I decided to just do it, I said to myself—you know, this Russia thing with Trump and Russia is a made-up story."[49]

A week later, the *New York Times* reported that Trump told a similar story to Russian ambassador Sergey Kislyak the day after Comey's dismissal. "I just fired the head of the F.B.I. He was crazy, a real nut job," Trump said at the official Oval Office meeting. "I faced great pressure because of Russia. That's taken off." The story was accompanied by a Russian Foreign Ministry photo of the dapper, blue-suited Kislyak laughing appreciatively at the president's joke.[50] American journalists were barred from the meeting, but the Russian delegation was allowed to bring a photographer.

Trump's meeting with Kislyak took place on May 10. On May 16, the *New York Times* reported that the president had asked James Comey to drop the investigation of Michael Flynn. The following day, Deputy Attorney General Rod Rosenstein announced the appointment of Robert Mueller as special counsel. In this capacity, Mueller would be responsible for investigating Russian interference with the 2016 presidential election and any other matters directly arising from that investigation. Mueller's appointment letter also specifically authorized him to investigate any criminal interference with his own investigation, including obstruction of justice.[51]

Trump was furious. Why wasn't Jeff Sessions protecting him the way Bobby Kennedy had protected JFK and Eric Holder had protected Barack Obama? Wasn't that what an attorney general was for? "Where is my Roy Cohn?" he demanded. The reference was to Joe McCarthy's legendarily vicious lieutenant, who also served as Trump's personal attorney and mentor in the president's younger days. If Trump had known that Sessions would recuse himself from the Russia inquiry, he never would have appointed him. "I wish I hadn't!" he tweeted.

During the next year, Trump's frustrations repeatedly boiled over in vitriolic Twitter fusillades. With startling ferocity and bile, he attacked both Sessions and Rosenstein for their role in perpetuating "the single greatest WITCH HUNT in American political history." Privately, Trump repeatedly but unsuccessfully badgered Sessions to reverse his recusal. At least once, he ordered the attorney general fired. He also tried to dismiss Robert Mueller at least twice but was talked down by the subordinates he directed to carry out the order.[52]

The Centrality of Motive

This episode, too, sheds important light on a president's ability to commit obstruction of justice. In broad outline, Donald Trump's pattern of behavior looks much like Richard Nixon's. But a great deal depends on the president's motives. Trump obviously sought to influence and impede the Russia investigations of both the FBI and Robert Mueller. The important and difficult question is why he took these actions.[53]

Trump's public statements strongly suggest that his official justification for firing James Comey was pretextual. They also strongly suggest that Comey's dismissal and Trump's later efforts to undermine Mueller were motivated by hostility to the Russia investigation. Beyond that, the available evidence is open to several plausible and potentially overlapping interpretations. One is that Trump was simply engaged in political damage control. A second is that he was motivated by personal vanity—specifically, his long-standing outrage at the scandal hanging over his 2016 election victory. A third is that Trump wanted to shut down the Russia investigation before it exposed his guilt or that of his family and friends. A fourth is that he expected the Justice Department to protect him and attack his enemies and was attempting to remake it in this mold. A fifth is that he sincerely believed the Russia investigation was a partisan vendetta with no legitimate factual or legal basis.

If any combination of the first four interpretations is correct, then Trump pretty clearly acted for an improper, purely selfish purpose. In that case, he very likely committed the crime of obstruction of justice. If the fifth interpretation is correct, then the question becomes substantially murkier. A president faced with a true "deep state" conspiracy to bring down his administration for nefarious reasons would certainly be justified in acting against it. Even a president who reasonably, but falsely, believed that he faced such a conspiracy would not commit a crime by attempting to suppress it. What about a president who maliciously deludes himself into this belief? This poses a much harder question, one that no court has ever come close to answering.[54]

Finally, there is the lingering question of whether a president is capable of obstructing justice when exercising his constitutional powers to supervise federal law enforcement. A substantial majority of legal scholars who have examined this question believe the answer is yes. History and logic support this view. Many lawyers and legal scholars have further concluded that Donald Trump in fact committed obstruction of justice. The arguments offered by these lawyers and scholars are important, as are those offered on the other side. But in the end, these questions are not likely to be decided in the courts or even on the basis of traditional legal arguments. That is because no special prosecutor is likely to indict a sitting president. The real question, in this case and in general, is whether Congress can be persuaded to impeach and convict a president on the ground of obstruction of justice.[55]

Experience suggests that the answer is yes, in the right circumstances. Whether those circumstances exist depends, like so much else, on the vigilance of the American people. Traditional legal arguments may help to stimulate popular awareness and to dispense with casuistic defenses of presidential misconduct. But the ultimate questions are deeper and more serious. Has the president sought to place himself above the law and do the American people care enough to do something about it? Only when the answer to both questions is yes is our constitutional system capable of holding a president accountable for obstruction of justice.

9

Can Congress Protect Special Prosecutors from the President?

There is something deeply strange about the American system for investigating presidents and high-level executive officials. The whole purpose of a special prosecutor is to investigate the president and his close allies independently and impartially. But the president has the power to fire a special prosecutor at any time. This looks a lot like the president investigating himself, contrary to the ancient maxim "No man shall be a judge in his own case." In more modern parlance, it seems to be a clear case of the fox guarding the henhouse.

After Watergate, the apparent oddity of this arrangement led Congress to pass the independent counsel statute. When that statute lapsed in 1999, the Justice Department adopted regulations that prohibit the firing of a special counsel without good reason. But those regulations can be repealed at any time at the direction of the president. They also cannot be enforced in court. To that extent, they perpetuate the oddity, rather than resolve it.

In April 2018, a bipartisan group of senators proposed legislation that would codify the special counsel regulations into law. If enacted, this proposal would also provide for judicial review when a special counsel is dismissed. Such legislation would help to resolve the oddity of the president investigating himself. But it would also raise an important and vexing question: Can Congress constitutionally restrict the president's power to remove a special prosecutor?[1]

The question arises because article II of the U.S. Constitution grants the president alone "the executive power of the United States." In plain English, the president is in charge of federal law enforcement, which includes the prosecution of federal crimes. Many thoughtful commentators believe the president can only exercise this power effectively if he possesses unlimited authority to fire any official with significant law enforcement responsibility. Special prosecutors certainly fit the bill. If these commentators are right, any congressional attempt to restrict the president's power to dismiss special prosecutors would be unconstitutional.[2]

Advocates of statutory protection for special prosecutors argue that the Constitution should be understood more flexibly. Historically, many federal prosecutions were handled by private attorneys. These attorneys operated with little or no meaningful supervision by the president or any other senior executive branch official. The attorney general, who serves at the pleasure of the president, did not exercise centralized control over federal prose-cutions until the early twentieth century. Could such a recent inno-vation really be compelled by the Constitution?

There is another important consideration. Under the Consitution's necessary and proper clause, Congress has authority to pass appropriate laws for implementing the powers of the exec-utive branch. Without this authority, none of the administrative architecture of federal law enforcement—neither the FBI nor the Justice Department—would exist at all. What Congress hath given, Congress can take away. If Congress could abolish the Justice Department and FBI altogether, surely it can impose modest restraints on the president's power to remove a special prosecutor. Or so the argument goes.[3]

Most important, as Supreme Court justice Robert Jackson famously wrote, the Constitution's checks and balances were intended to establish "a workable government." When Congress prohibits the president from capriciously firing a special prosecutor, it does not seize any law enforcement power for itself. Under recent proposals, Congress has no role in choosing the special prosecutor or deciding whether a particular special prosecutor should be dismissed. It merely establishes a much-needed check on the president's power to act as a judge in his own case. All of this, proponents argue, makes a statutorily protected special prosecutor perfectly consistent with the Constitution's practical conception of the separation of powers.[4]

In the 1988 case of *Morrison v. Olson*, the Supreme Court agreed. At that time, the independent counsel statute was just a decade old. Watergate was still a recent and painful memory, and a judicial decision striking down the statute was almost unthinkable. The independent counsel was difficult to square with the logic of the Court's earlier decisions, but pragmatism won out. The Court concluded that the statute did not "impermissibly interfere with the President's exercise of his constitutionally appointed functions." In other words, the president could still do the job the Constitution gave him. For seven of the eight justices who decided the case, that was enough. Only Justice Antonin Scalia dissented.[5]

The Court's decision disappointed hardcore legal conservatives, but most observers viewed it as sensible and pragmatic. At the time, Bill Clinton was serving his fourth two-year term as governor of Arkansas, after reluctantly sitting out the 1988 presidential primary. Clinton's future tormentor Kenneth Starr was comfortably ensconced as a life-tenured judge on the United States Court of Appeals. Monica Lewinsky was just fourteen years old. Most

Americans had never heard of any of them. Ten years later, all three would be household names. The Court's decision in *Morrison v. Olson* would come to look very different as a result.

Another Supreme Court Showdown

Independent counsel Alexia Morrison arrived at the Supreme Court on April 26, 1988, under overcast skies and a light drizzle. The scene was far more sedate than the last time a special prosecutor tangled with the president in the nation's highest court. No cheering throngs greeted Morrison. No one shouted "Give 'em hell, Alexia baby!" Yet the stakes were nearly as high on this blustery spring day as they had been in the summer of 1974. The future of the independent counsel hung in the balance. Lawyers and Washington insiders understood this, and a substantial line had formed outside the Court early that morning. Former Justice Department lawyer Theodore Olson, the man challenging the constitutionality of the independent counsel, was among them. He had joined the queue at 5 a.m. to assure himself a seat.[6]

Four months earlier, almost to the day, the United States Court of Appeals had ruled the independent counsel statute unconstitutional. This decision threatened more than Alexia Morrison's investigation of Theodore Olson for lying to Congress. There were three other ongoing independent counsel investigations, including Lawrence Walsh's much higher profile probe of the Iran-Contra affair. More broadly, the Court of Appeals decision struck at the heart of the nation's post-Watergate consensus that president could not be trusted to investigate his own administration. It would now be up to Morrison to defend that consensus. She would be doing so on the nation's biggest legal stage and against two of the most accomplished appellate lawyers in the country.[7]

As she climbed the marble steps to the Supreme Court, the weight of responsibility resting on Morrison's shoulders was immense. At forty, she would be arguing her first case before the justices. She had rejected the advice of many friends and colleagues to hand over the reins to an experienced Supreme Court specialist. This was no time, they had argued, for learning the ropes. What if she froze up under the klieg lights of the Supreme Court chamber? Besides, the justices would have no idea who she was. Morrison was an experienced federal prosecutor and former litigation chief for the Securities and Exchange Commission. But she had not clerked for the Supreme Court and had no reputation as an appellate advocate or constitutional expert. With so much on the line, most lawyers thought the argument should be handled by someone the justices already knew and trusted.[8]

Morrison saw their point. In some sense, it would have been a relief to relinquish responsibility for arguing the case. But she thought her "intimate familiarity with the statute and how it worked" was crucial. No hired gun would know the law as well as she did. Nor would any constitutional expert have the same credibility to explain to the justices how the law actually operated in practice. Eight days before the scheduled argument, her nine-year-old daughter Amanda came down with chicken pox. Morrison had visions of standing before the justices with itchy red welts covering her face. But she quickly put such thoughts—and all other distractions—out of her mind. She was the independent counsel, and she would have to shoulder the burden of defending the statute that established her authority.[9]

Morrison's principal adversary at the Court that day would be Solicitor General Charles Fried. Angular and birdlike in appearance, with piercingly inquisitive eyes, Fried was one of the nation's most distinguished professors of constitutional law. During his tenure as the government's top Supreme Court lawyer, he had argued before the justices more than twenty times. On top of his greater experience, Fried would enjoy the elevated stature of his position as "the Tenth Justice." This moniker for the solicitor general is somewhat misleading, since the office has always been a political one. But the name has this much going for it: the Office of the Solicitor General wins the vast majority of its cases—and not just by coincidence. Studies have shown that the solicitor general's views carry significantly greater weight with the justices than those of other litigants. Morrison would have her work cut out for her.[10]

As usual, the argument was scheduled to begin at 10 a.m. Each side would have forty-five minutes to make its case. This was 50 percent longer than the time allotted in a typical case. But it was only half as long as the justices had allowed for Leon Jaworski's clash with Richard Nixon. As the party who had sought Supreme Court review, Alexia Morrison would argue first. She would be followed by Michael Davidson, a lawyer for the Senate, who would join her in defending the independent counsel statute. Then the opposing side would have its turn. Thomas Martin, the tall, handsome Justice Department veteran representing Theodore Olson, would argue first. After Martin finished, Solicitor General Fried would argue against the constitutionality of the independent counsel on behalf of President Reagan. Morrison would then have a final opportunity for rebuttal.

The stage was set for round 2 of the special prosecutor versus the president. Ronald Reagan was not formally a party to the case. But the solicitor general's presence made clear that much more was at stake than the investigation of a former assistant attorney general. Lawrence Walsh's Iran-Contra investigation loomed large over the entire proceedings. It was an ominous reminder that a different independent counsel might some day be called on to investigate the alleged crimes of a president. Charles Fried arrived at the

Supreme Court with one overriding mission—to head that possibility off at the pass. A well-prepared and resolute Alexia Morrison would try to stop him.

The Back Story

In early 1980s Washington, revolution was in the air. A conservative insurgent, Ronald Reagan had snatched the Republican presidential nomination from establishment favorite George H. W. Bush. He then won a decisive victory over Jimmy Carter in the 1980 election. In contrast to the moderate approach of his recent Republican predecessors, Reagan promised radical change. He did not want to rein in or recalibrate the New Deal welfare and regulatory state. He wanted to dismantle it completely. Sunny, optimistic, and full of passionate conviction, the new president immediately set about cutting taxes and regulations with missionary zeal. His motto was simple: "government is not the solution to our problem; government is the problem." Reagan failed in his quest to overturn the New Deal. But nearly all scholars agree that he was a transformational president, who ushered in a fundamentally new era in American politics.[11]

He did not accomplish this alone. When Reagan arrived in Washington in January 1981, he brought with him a large train of followers. Like Reagan himself, these supporters viewed rolling back "big government" as a high moral calling. None held this belief more fervently than Anne M. Gorsuch, a forty-year-old former Colorado congresswoman and Reagan's first pick to head the Environmental Protection Agency. Strikingly attractive, with short dark hair and a partiality for pearl necklaces, Gorsuch also chain-smoked Marlboros and had a well-earned reputation for toughness. According to her hometown newspaper, she "could kick a bear to death with her bare feet."[12]

Upon assuming her new post, Gorsuch quickly gained a reputation as formidably intelligent, uncompromising, and ruthless. She was determined to tame—her critics said strangle—the agency she had been appointed to lead. During less than two years in office, Gorsuch reduced the agency's budget by over 20 percent and slashed environmental enforcement actions by 60 percent. She frequently boasted that she had "reduced the thickness of the book of clean water regulations from six inches to a half-inch."[13]

Unsurprisingly, neither agency employees nor congressional Democrats took kindly to this style of leadership. Environmental activists oscillated between hair-on-fire panic and apocalyptic despair. William Drayton, a former assistant EPA administrator, declared publicly that Gorsuch had "demolished the nation's environmental enforcement capacity." Two anonymous civil service employees penned a *New York Times* op-ed reporting that agency staff morale was "at a low ebb." They closed with a warning: "[I]t will be many years before the agency can recover from the spiritual and budgetary beatings it has taken."[14]

Congressional investigations followed in short order. The most intense and prolonged of them involved the Superfund program, a $1.6 billion fund established by Congress to clean up hazardous waste sites. Gorsuch herself was alleged to have delayed $6.1 million in Superfund aid to damage the U.S. Senate campaign of California governor Jerry Brown. Over lunch on the presidential yacht, *Sequoia*, two witnesses overheard Gorsuch remark, "I'll be damned if I am going to let Brown take credit for the cleanup."[15]

Eventually, a Justice Department probe would clear Gorsuch of any criminal misconduct. Meanwhile, the House of Representatives voted to subpoena hundreds of thousands of EPA documents. At the direction of President Reagan, Gorsuch refused to comply with the subpoena on grounds of executive privilege. To turn over the requested documents, she claimed, would jeopardize secret agency legal strategies for pursuing industrial polluters. Congressional critics alleged a cover-up, while the administration's defenders insisted that Reagan was simply protecting the institution of the presidency.

Behind the scenes, Gorsuch was acutely frustrated at being dragged into a clash with Congress. In her view, the Justice Department lawyers advising EPA "had tremendous egos" and mostly "wanted to make a name for themselves in Washington." Gorsuch and her deputies repeatedly told the Justice Department that turning over the requested documents would cause no appreciable harm to the agency, but publicly she toed the administration line.[16]

Quickly, the situation mushroomed into something approaching a constitutional crisis. Frustrated with the administration's stonewalling, the House voted to hold Gorsuch in contempt of Congress and sought to have her arrested on this charge. After two tense months, the standoff ended with a whimper when the White House agreed to turn over the subpoenaed documents. In exchange, the House withdrew the contempt charge against Gorsuch. Immediately thereafter, Anne Gorsuch resigned under pressure from the White House, feeling cruelly and callously abandoned for the crime of doing the president's "dirty work."[17]

It's the Cover-Up, Again

Congress, however, was not yet prepared to let the matter rest. In the view of many Democratic House members, the Reagan administration had engaged in a sustained campaign to obstruct their investigation of the EPA. They suspected a cover-up orchestrated by the Justice Department and asked the House Judiciary Committee to investigate. Judiciary chairman Peter Rodino, the

Democratic doyen who presided over the Nixon impeachment hearings, happily obliged.[18]

On March 10, 1983, the Committee called assistant attorney general Theodore Olson as a witness. Sandy-haired, with perpetually amused eyes and a wry grin, Olson was among the most brilliant lawyers of his generation. He was also a staunch conservative of the new breed that descended on Washington in droves after Reagan's victory. Based on these qualifications, he was tapped to head the Office of Legal Counsel, a low-profile but crucially important division of the Justice Department. In this capacity, Olson had served as principal architect of EPA's legal argument for resisting the subpoena issued by the House of Representatives.

Still incensed at this stonewalling, the members of the House Judiciary Committee wanted answers. Where did this forty-two-year-old lawyer get the audacity to defy a lawful order from the Congress of the United States? Wasn't he ashamed of himself for giving such bad legal advice? Were there still things he and the Justice Department were hiding from the Committee? On multiple occasions, Representative John Seiberling of Ohio, a fierce environmentalist, roughly chastised Olson for not having the "good grace" to resign. "If I had a lawyer that gave me advice that led to an absolute disaster," Seiberling said, "I would get another lawyer. I think this is one of those situations. If I were the President, that's what I would do."[19]

Over several hours of intense questioning, Olson gave numerous answers that congressional investigators later judged to be false and misleading. In particular, investigators believed Olson had sought to conceal thousands of pages of undisclosed drafts that should have been turned over to Congress. They also accused him of lying about his role in providing legal advice to EPA.[20] These alleged lies were painstakingly documented in a three-thousand-page Committee report published in 1985.

Following publication of the report, Judiciary chairman Rodino formally requested that the attorney general appoint an independent counsel to investigate. After the ninety-day preliminary inquiry required by the independent counsel statute, department investigators found substantial evidence that Olson had knowingly lied to Congress. Constrained by this conclusion, Attorney General Edwin Meese reluctantly asked the Court of Appeals to appoint an independent counsel. The Court selected Alexia Morrison, who promptly served Olson with a grand jury subpoena to produce documents relevant to her investigation. Just as promptly, Olson challenged the constitutionality of the statute authorizing Morrison's appointment.[21]

This was no off-the-cuff, wing-and-a-prayer defense strategy. Top conservative lawyers and legal intellectuals—including Olson himself—had long argued that the independent counsel statute was unconstitutional. In 1981, Reagan's first attorney general, William French Smith, expressed this view formally in correspondence with the Senate. By 1987, when Olson first raised his constitutional challenge, the Reagan administration had assiduously staffed the federal courts with conservative judges. Most of those judges shared Reagan's broad views of presidential power. When Reagan signed the independent counsel statute that year, he noted his constitutional objections to the law in a signing statement. Olson had been intimately and personally involved with many of these efforts. He now had an intimate and personal reason to hope they would bear fruit.[22]

The Marvelous Ms. Morrison

The eight black-robed justices who filed into the Supreme Court shortly after 10 a.m. on April 26, 1988, were a different group from the one that decided *United States v. Nixon*. William Rehnquist, the former Justice Department lawyer who was brand new to the Court in 1974, now occupied the chief justice's chair, elevated to that position by Ronald Reagan. Potter Stewart and William O. Douglas, the two justices who had questioned Richard Nixon's lawyer most aggressively, were dead. Lewis Powell had just retired, as had Chief Justice Warren Burger, who wrote the Court's opinion in the *Nixon* case.

Taking their places were Sandra Day O'Connor, the first woman ever to serve on the Supreme Court, and Antonin Scalia, a former University of Chicago law professor. In just two years, Scalia had already established himself as the Court's most forceful and acerbic conservative voice. Justice Anthony Kennedy had been confirmed by the Senate two months earlier. But he had recused himself for unspecified reasons and was not present. Rounding out the Court was John Paul Stevens, a bow-tied Chicago Republican who increasingly voted with the Court's liberals. He had joined the Court in 1975. All told, President Reagan had appointed three of the eight justices who would decide the independent counsel's—and Theodore Olson's—fate. Two of them, Antonin Scalia and William Rehnquist, had previously held the same job as Olson at the Office of Legal Counsel.

Balding and somewhat owlish in appearance, the chief justice bent to the microphone before him. Not yet sporting the gold epaulets he would adopt in the mid-1990s, to some snickering, Rehnquist wore a traditional plain black robe. The small knot of a paisley tie protruded slightly from its throat. His plastic, aviator-framed glasses gave him a conspicuously unstylish appearance even for a Supreme Court justice, which he seemed to relish. After briefly announcing the case, he invited Alexia Morrison to commence her argument. "Ms. Morrison, you may begin whenever you are ready."[23]

Morrison rose from her seat at the counsel table and took two steps left toward the podium. With her auburn hair pulled back in a loose bun, she was an exceptional sight in the Supreme Court chamber. Today, women still amount to barely 15 percent of the lawyers arguing before the Court. In 1988, the number was even lower. Morrison, however, could not afford to dwell on this fact one way or another. She had a case to argue, one of surpassing importance not only to her own work but also to the country as a whole. Through large, dark-framed glasses, she took a final glance at her notes. It was time. On the counsel table beside her, next to the goose-quill pens that each lawyer received as a keepsake, lay a battered and heavily creased sheet of notepaper. In her daughter's childish scrawl, it read simply, "I love you very, very much."[24]

"Mr. Chief Justice, and may it please the Court," Morrison began. Her voice was strong and clear, wavering just slightly as she warmed to her task. "The question before you," she said, "concerns whether the independent counsel provisions of the Ethics in Government Act run afoul of the Constitution of the United States." She proceeded to describe how the case had arrived at the Supreme Court and to lay out the history of the independent counsel statute. She particularly emphasized that both houses of Congress and the president had extensively considered and endorsed the law on three separate occasions—first when it was originally adopted in 1978 and then again when it was reauthorized in 1983 and 1987.[25]

Like the justices, every member of Congress who voted for the law had sworn an oath to support the Constitution. Presidents Carter and Reagan, who signed the law, had sworn an even stronger oath to "preserve, protect, and defend the Constitution." The Supreme Court would have to make its own decision about the constitutionality of the independent counsel. But Morrison plainly hoped the justices would agree with the great chief justice

John Marshall, who had written, in a similar case in 1819: "it would require no ordinary share of intrepidity to assert that a measure adopted under these circumstances was a bold and plain usurpation to which the Constitution gave no countenance." Tactfully, Morrison chose not to quote these words directly. One does not accuse Supreme Court justices of "intrepidity" to their faces. But no one steeped in U.S. constitutional history could fail to hear their echo in her argument.[26]

Moving on, still without interruption by the justices, Morrison crisply and precisely summarized the process for appointing an independent counsel. Studiously neutral in tone, she nevertheless subtly focused the Court's attention on the central premise of her constitutional defense: Congress had reserved no power to itself to control or supervise the independent counsel or even to determine whether one should be appointed. Nor did Congress assign any such power to the courts. Rather, these powers remained wholly with the attorney general, an official hand-picked by the president and subject to removal by him at any time. The statute also empowered the attorney general, not the courts or Congress, to remove the independent counsel, though this authority could only be exercised for "good cause."[27]

The justices allowed Morrison to speak at some length about the structure of the statute. They then peppered her with rapid-fire questions about how the law operated in practice. Here, her intimate familiarity with the statute paid off in spades. She answered expertly and dispassionately, confining herself to the precise language of the statute, its historical application, and her firsthand experience operating under it. Her responses were never argumentative or oratorical. Yet she deftly exploited the justices' curiosity to cast the independent counsel statute in the most reasonable possible light. As Morrison described them, independent counsels were simply ordinary federal prosecutors, bound by established

Justice Department policies. Like other prosecutors, they were subject to oversight by the attorney general. The only difference was a few modest additional safeguards established by Congress to eliminate the appearance or the reality of a conflict of interest.[28]

When the questions briefly turned to matters of abstract constitutional principle, Morrison proved somewhat less sure-footed. But on the whole, she turned in a masterful performance. Her intuition had been correct. The justices were most interested in the nuts and bolts of the independent counsel statute. No Supreme Court specialist could have fielded their questions on this front more ably—or with greater credibility—than Morrison had done. Often, the best constitutional defense of a challenged law is a sympathetic description of its provisions and aims. The Supreme Court novice Alexia Morrison had offered a master class in this strategy.[29]

Mr. Fried Takes Up the Gauntlet

The Court next heard from Michael Davidson, representing the U.S. Senate, and Thomas Martin, representing Theodore Olson. Davidson argued in support of the independent counsel and Martin in opposition. Both gave competent, if workmanlike, performances. But their time at the podium felt like an intermission between the two main acts of the high constitutional drama at hand. When Martin sat down, the chief justice announced, "We'll now hear from you, General Fried."[30]

On that cue, solicitor general Charles Fried rose to the podium. Looking almost sepulchral in his long-tailed morning coat, he proceeded to offer his own master class in a starkly contrasting style of argument—what might be called "high constitutional oratory." Ordinarily, the justices are unmoved by passionate invocations of abstract ideals. "General propositions," Justice Oliver Wendell Holmes famously wrote, "do not decide concrete cases."

Besides, Supreme Court justices like to think of themselves as analytical rather than emotional creatures. Yet in sufficiently expert hands, the Constitution can be made to sing in a register that moves even the stony breasts and flinty minds of Supreme Court justices. Charles Fried possessed such hands. In barely ten minutes at the podium, he made the case against the independent counsel far more forcefully than Thomas Martin had managed in twice that amount of time.[31]

"Our central objection," he began, "is that this statute strips the President of a purely executive function and lodges that function in one almost wholly untethered to the President." To make matters worse, Fried continued, the independent counsel statute "absolves the Congress of its weightiest and most painful duty, which is the scrutiny of the Executive Branch, backed up by the painful duty of impeachment." There was the case against the independent counsel, wrapped up with a nice neat bow. The Constitution commands that criminal prosecution be carried out under the supervision of a democratically elected president. If the president fails in his responsibilities, the only constitutional remedy is impeachment by a democratically elected Congress.[32]

Knowing that Watergate would be on the justices' minds, Fried immediately attempted to turn that traumatic episode to his advantage. "True," he conceded, "the dismissal of Special Prosecutor Cox was regrettable, but it was not a constitutional catastrophe." Another special prosecutor, Leon Jaworski, had immediately been appointed and allowed to pursue his work to its conclusion. The system had worked. It did so, Fried pointed out, "not because of jury-rigged constitutional innovations, but because of public pressure and the long, deep shadow of Congress's power of impeachment." This brought the solicitor general to the height of his formidable eloquence: "it is the central fallacy of this statute to think that a supremely political object can be accomplished without politics."[33]

At this point in his argument, constitutional principle and practical wisdom merged. A special prosecutor, Fried argued, is not an "automaton who mechanically processes evidence and law. What is involved is judgment. What is involved is discretion. That kind of judgment, that kind of discretion, can only be safely lodged in somebody who is responsible to an elected official, who is subject to Congressional oversight, and if need be, impeachment." Fried's dazzling performance provoked only two perfunctory questions, both in the closing minutes of his argument. Afterward, he saw this as an evil omen that the justices had already made up their minds. In any event, his efforts had been for naught. He had not persuaded them.[34]

Justice Scalia Dissents

The Supreme Court handed down its decision upholding the independent counsel on June 27, 1988. Justice Scalia registered a lonely and impassioned dissent, which he took the unusual step of reading from the bench. He did so, he said, because he thought *Morrison v. Olson* "one of the most important opinions the Court has issued in many years." It did not involve "any of the wonderful guarantees of our Bill of Rights," but he urged the American people not to be fooled. "In the dictatorships of the modern world, Bills of Rights are a dime a dozen. What makes ours work is a governmental structure, a constitution of government designed by 55 extraordinarily wise national leaders" in the summer of 1787. This structure, he said, was the most vital constitutional safeguard of liberty. By upholding the independent counsel statute, the Court had placed that structure in serious jeopardy.[35]

Scalia's dissenting opinion in *Morrison*—perhaps the most famous he ever wrote—makes many intricate and technical legal arguments. At its heart, however, is a deeply practical concern: the power of a federal prosecutor cannot be safely entrusted to an official who is not accountable to any elected politician. Echoing Charles Fried, Scalia emphasized that prosecution does not simply involve the mechanical application of law to facts. Rather, prosecutors in the American system wield enormous discretionary power, which requires some kind of check against abuse.[36]

To make this point, Scalia quoted the eloquent statement of Supreme Court justice and former attorney general Robert Jackson: "one of the greatest difficulties of the position of prosecutor is that he must pick his cases, because no prosecutor can investigate all of the cases in which he receives complaints. If the prosecutor is obliged to choose his case, it follows that he can choose his defendants. Therein is the most dangerous power of the prosecutor—that he will pick people that he thinks he should get, rather than cases that need to be prosecuted." For Scalia, it was chilling to contemplate handing this awesome power to an independent counsel who was, by design, accountable to no one.[37]

Scalia could not believe that his colleagues would allow such a blatant perversion of the constitutional design to go unchallenged. "Frequently," he observed, "an issue of this sort will come before the Court clad in sheep's clothing. The potential to effect important change is not immediately evident and must be discerned by a careful and perceptive analysis. But this wolf comes as a wolf." Near the end of his life, Scalia would still recall *Morrison v. Olson* as "the most wrenching" case of his three-decade Supreme Court career.[38]

In 1988, Justice Scalia stood alone. Ten years later, following the ill-fated independent counsel investigation of President Clinton, Scalia's dire predictions came to seem spectacularly prescient.

Every danger he warned of had been realized—an out-of-control independent counsel, monomaniacally focused on bringing down a particular defendant, with no competing demands on his time and no superior to rein in his excesses. As former solicitor general Walter Dellinger colorfully put it in 1998, "the parade of horribles envisioned by Justice Scalia is now marching right down Pennsylvania Avenue." When Congress allowed the independent counsel to lapse in 1999, many observers interpreted its decision as a tacit ratification of Scalia's constitutional argument.[39]

Over time, this understanding became widespread. As Harvard law professor Adrian Vermeule explains, "a bipartisan judgment had formed that the Independent Counsel was a kind of constitutional Frankenstein's monster." By 2018, two former solicitors general writing in the *New York Times* could casually take Scalia's position for granted. "It would probably be unconstitutional," they wrote in passing, for Congress to protect special counsel Robert Mueller against capricious dismissal. In expressing this opinion, they did not feel compelled even to mention that *Morrison v. Olson* had expressly and lopsidedly ruled the contrary. One of the two former solicitors general who wrote this statement was Kenneth Starr.[40]

For this reason and for reasons of ordinary politics, Congress seems unlikely to pass legislation protecting special prosecutors any time soon. This could be for the best. It probably renders a repeat of the Starr investigation's excesses less likely. On the other hand, the reaction to those excesses looks somewhat overheated in retrospect, and the problem of foxes guarding henhouses remains frighteningly real. In any event, the responsibility for protecting special prosecutors now rests where it has for most of U.S. history—squarely on the shoulders of the American people.

Epilogue

A Double-Edged Sword

The history and law of special prosecutors teach a single over-arching lesson. The rule of law is as strong as the American people choose to make it—and no stronger. In some sense, this is heartening. It is also a sobering reminder. The democratic institutions and traditions handed down by previous generations are not indestructible. Like any other inheritance, they can be squandered, and there are real reasons to fear we are doing just that. In these unsettled times, special prosecutors might serve as highly visible catalysts bulwarks for democracy. Or they might be swept asunder by the flood tides of populism and political polarization. These large structural forces are central features of contemporary American politics, and they do not bode well. But scratch the surface, and those forces are revealed to comprise millions of individual citizens with minds of their own. The choices of those individuals—*our* choices—will determine the fate of constitutional democracy in America. This is not hyperbole. It is a simple statement of fact.

Historically, special prosecutor investigations have followed two broad patterns. In the best-case scenario, politics functions as a one-way ratchet reinforcing presidential accountability. At the outset, political pressure forces the president to appoint special prosecutors to investigate serious allegations against themselves or their close associates. Once appointed, a special prosecutor gives those allegations new salience and serves as a convenient focal point for public monitoring of the president. This makes it politically costly for the president to impede a special prosecutor's investigation and positively toxic for the president to fire a special prosecutor. Meanwhile, a special prosecutor buys time and freedom to carry out a thorough investigation.

If that investigation turns up significant evidence of high-level wrongdoing, it becomes even more costly for the president to interfere. If the president is bold or foolish enough to fire the special prosecutor under these circumstances, the decision is highly likely to backfire. In that event, the appointment of a new and equally tenacious replacement might be the only way for the president to avoid impeachment. Even this might not be enough.

This is the best-case scenario, but the worst-case scenario has been at least equally common. The same political dynamic that empowers special prosecutors gives the president powerful incentives to destroy their credibility, if he can pull it off. The more successful such attacks are, the lower the political price a president will pay for stonewalling or interfering with the special prosecutor's investigation. He might even get away with firing the special prosecutor.

In pursuing such a strategy, presidents benefit greatly from the limited expertise and attention span of most ordinary citizens. Often, a presidential scandal will simply be too complicated for much of the public to follow. Even if the scandal is not especially complicated, the president can usually generate the illusion of complexity, through a calculated misinformation campaign. Ordinary citizens are not stupid or gullible. Few, however, have the time or interest to follow such matters closely. Even if the public had direct, unmediated access to the facts, it would be difficult for most ordinary citizens to digest the information sufficiently to form an intelligent judgment. This becomes much harder when highly skilled and lavishly funded professionals are working on both sides to massage the facts to their political advantage.

Several conditions make the worst-case scenario more likely. If the president's party controls one or both houses of Congress, the deterrent power of impeachment is far lower. If the president is nearing the end of his tenure he will generally be less susceptible to political pressure because he has little to lose. If the president is broadly popular or benefits from a strong partisan media apparatus he can withstand far more political adversity than a president who does not enjoy these advantages. If all or most of these circumstances are present simultaneously, some version of the worst-case scenario is the likeliest outcome. Such is the double-edged sword of democratic politics.

A Republic, If We Can Keep It

In any given case, supporters of the president's party will naturally root for the special prosecutor to fail. Supporters of the opposing party will naturally do the opposite. To some extent, this is unavoidable. But all Americans should understand that the special prosecutor *as an institution* is nonpartisan. For well over a century, presidents from both major parties have appointed special prosecutors. Their function is one in which all Americans have a profound stake—to ensure that presidents and other high officials are held legally accountable. Anyone who favors this result only for presidents of the opposite party has abandoned the rule of law. For that high ideal to survive, some substantial fraction of the American people must be willing to hold a president of their own party accountable for breaking the law. Otherwise, we as a nation will have cast our lot with Thrasymachus, the antihero of Plato's *Republic*, for whom justice is "nothing but the advantage of the stronger."[1]

Of course, special prosecutors are not the only actors in our constitutional system capable of checking presidential abuse. In various ways, the courts, Congress, and even the federal bureaucracy also perform this function—or can perform it, if they so choose. But if these other institutions are to do their jobs, the people need an alert system—a fire alarm or a canary in the coal mine. Otherwise, they will not know when to press their elected representatives and other institutional checks into action. At their best, special prosecutors play this role very effectively, but it is just a first step. Special prosecutors can expose the president's wrongdoing, but they cannot make the American people care. That part is up to us. To paraphrase Benjamin Franklin, the founders gave us a republic. Only we can keep it.

This is not an easy job. Special prosecutors, like presidents, sometimes abuse their authority, lose their sense of proportion, or both. When the president is a member of one's own party, it is all too tempting to believe that this is the case. Sometimes it actually will be, but history counsels skepticism. Since the birth of special prosecutors in 1875, this charge has been leveled with extraordinary promiscuity. Only rarely has it had a substantial basis in reality. In any case, for special prosecutors to perform their vital role, a substantial fraction of the people must put aside partisanship and judge their performance on its merits.

The Best-Case Scenario

If this seems like an impossibly tall order, consider the case of Watergate. In November of 1972, Richard Nixon won nearly 18 million more votes than George McGovern. In absolute terms, this was the largest popular vote margin in U.S. history. When Nixon took the oath of office on January 20, 1973, an overwhelming 67 percent of the public approved of his performance in office. Twenty months later, Nixon resigned in disgrace after a special prosecutor investigation demonstrated his complicity in a sordid conspiracy to obstruct justice. He did not abdicate his office out of shame; even at the bitter end, he showed little remorse for his actions. Rather, the people, and then Nixon's congressional allies, had abandoned him—not every last one of them, but enough. By August 8, 1974, the day he resigned, Nixon's public approval rating had fallen to 24 percent. Well over half of those who voted for him two years earlier had changed their minds when faced with clear evidence of his criminal activity.[2]

How did this happen? Special prosecutors Archibald Cox and Leon Jaworski were a big part of the story. Their highly salient investigation and courtroom victories generated the political pressure that forced Nixon to turn over his secret White House tapes. The tapes, in turn, exposed Nixon's direct involvement in the Watergate cover-up. Archibald Cox's news conference on the afternoon of the Saturday Night Massacre helped the American people understand the gravity of Nixon's lawlessness. This was not enough to save Cox, but it forced Nixon to appoint another credible special prosecutor to succeed him. Leon Jaworski's victory at the Supreme Court in July 1974 delivered the coup de grâce. After the Court's ruling, Nixon had no choice but to release his "smoking gun" conversation with Haldeman on June 23, 1972. From that point, his resignation was only a matter of time.

Cox and Jaworski, however, were lucky. They benefited from an unusually favorable concatenation of circumstances. Democratic congressional majorities and an effective news media were especially important. It was Watergate burglar James McCord's testimony before the Senate that prompted the appointment of a special prosecutor in the first place. The televised Senate hearings

in June 1973—especially John Dean's testimony at those hearings—
placed Watergate at the center of public consciousness. The following summer, televised impeachment hearings before the House
Judiciary Committee helped keep Watergate in the public eye after
many long months of scandal. Finally, the looming threat of impeachment played a decisive role in driving Nixon from office.[3]

Without a vigilant and broadly trusted news media, there
might have been no occasion for a serious congressional investigation. Without Democratic control of Congress, Nixon's allies
might have blocked such an investigation before it got started.
And without saturation coverage of the House and Senate hearings on the major television networks, Watergate might never have
captured the nation's attention. Even with all these advantages, the
special prosecutor investigation might still have ended in partisan
stalemate without the spectacular gift of Nixon's secret tapes.[4]

Despite these caveats, the special prosecutor investigation of
Watergate accomplished something extraordinary. A popular
president, fresh off a landslide election victory, was forced from
office by a special prosecutor he could have fired at any time.
Nixon thought the laws made for ordinary people did not apply
to the president. Leon Jaworski and Archibald Cox taught him
otherwise. They never could have done so without the support of
the American people. Especially crucial were the tens of millions
of Nixon voters who put aside partisanship when the evidence
showed that the president was a crook.

The Worst-Case Scenario

Contrast Watergate with the Whiskey Ring scandal. At the time of
the latter, Ulysses Grant was a lame-duck president nearing the end
of his final term. As the scandal gained momentum, Democrats
won control the House of Representatives, but Grant's Republican

Party maintained a slim Senate majority. This effectively foreclosed the possibility of impeachment, especially for a scandal that never implicated Grant personally. The partisan Republican media apparatus also played a crucial role, vilifying special prosecutor John Henderson and defending the probity of Grant and his allies.[5]

This was a transitional period for the national media. Republican and Democratic party tribunes provided the usual intensely partisan coverage of the Whiskey Ring scandal. But other newspapers offered more independent coverage, much of it harshly critical of the Grant administration. This coverage played a major role in forcing Grant to appoint a special prosecutor. It also helped to keep John Henderson in office even as he indicted dozens of Whiskey Ring conspirators, including Grant's wartime associate John McDonald. On the other hand, the absence of a robust, broadly trusted, independent news media gave Grant far freer rein than he would have enjoyed in later periods.[6]

For all of these reasons, Grant could afford to take the political heat for firing Henderson. He did feel compelled to appoint another special prosecutor, but under the circumstances, this did little to repair the damage. John Henderson was far more knowledgeable about the Whiskey Ring investigation than anyone else. By firing him on the eve of Orville Babcock's trial, Grant threw the entire prosecution into disarray. With Babcock in the crosshairs, Grant further got away with testifying on his friend's behalf. This unprecedented maneuver subverted the prosecution quite as effectively as a direct order shutting it down. It did not help that Grant was a political naïf ensconced in a cocoon of intensely partisan and paranoid supporters.[7]

John Henderson's investigation was not a complete failure. It exposed public corruption on a vast scale. It brought dozens of corrupt officeholders and their accomplices to justice. In the process, it raised the salience of good government as a political issue. This almost certainly cost the Republican Party dearly in the 1876 election cycle. Ordinarily, that would be a good thing. All else equal, democracy works best when official corruption is met with swift and severe political punishment. In 1876, however, Republican control of the federal government was the only barrier protecting newly emancipated black Americans from a reign of white racial terrorism.

By tarnishing the Republican brand, the Whiskey Ring scandal hastened the end of Reconstruction. In doing so, it helped to cement a reconciliation of North and South premised on the continued subjugation of black Americans. In this sense, both the Republican Party and the nation paid a terrible price for Grant's complacent toleration of corruption. Unlike Richard Nixon, however, neither Orville Babcock nor Ulysses Grant was ever forced to answer personally for his subversion of the rule of law. Corruption remained endemic in American government for several decades to come.[8]

Could a president ever get away with firing a special prosecutor today? The answer is clearly yes. Bill Clinton might well have fired Ken Starr, arguably with good reason, if the independent counsel statute had not protected him against removal. The attacks Clinton's allies launched against Starr's team were relentless, vicious, and devastatingly effective with the public. Thanks to a booming economy, Clinton actually grew in popularity during Starr's investigation. It is highly probable that he could have survived the fallout of firing Starr.

Now that the independent counsel statute has lapsed, the Justice Department regulations that replaced it still provide some residual security. They publicly commit the president not to fire a special prosecutor without good reason. They also require the attorney general to notify senior congressional leadership of both parties of the reasons for a special prosecutor's dismissal. Reinforced by broad public support, these restraints might prove quite powerful, as similar restraints did during Watergate. Without such support, they seem exceedingly unlikely to constrain a determined president.

To say once more that the ultimate outcome depends on the American people may seem like a gauzy cliché. It is also a simple fact—not a particularly reassuring one, given present circumstances. These are unsteady times, by any measure. Leading commentators widely lament the tribalist state of American politics, the loss of public trust in established institutions, and the decay of democratic norms. Partisan media outlets are stronger and the mainstream media weaker than at any time in recent memory. Are the American people, in this historical moment, capable of standing up to a lawless president? What if that president is backed by a friendly Congress and a hardcore base of popular support?

Cast in these terms, the likelihood seems low. Yet Watergate also occurred during unsteady times, and tens of millions of Americans who backed Nixon in 1972 managed to keep an open mind. When the chips were down, they had the courage and principle to stand up in defense of the special prosecutor's vital mission. Whether contemporary Americans can muster the same courage and principle will do much to determine the future of American democracy.

The Crucial Role of Norms

It is not mere happenstance that special prosecutors were more effective during Watergate than during the Whiskey Ring scandal one hundred years earlier. For a special prosecutor to generate significant political pressure on a president, the public must possess widely shared standards for acceptable presidential behavior. Those standards must also be high enough that interfering with or firing a special prosecutor would violate them. Legal scholars and social scientists call such standards "norms" or "conventions." Those norms and conventions were much thicker and more robust in the 1970s than they were in the 1870s, when corruption and graft bred widespread public cynicism about politics.[9]

This is a major reason why Richard Nixon's firing of Archibald Cox set off such an uproar. By 1973, the public possessed a strong and widely shared sense that serious allegations of presidential law-breaking should be investigated thoroughly and impartially. When Nixon violated this norm by firing Cox without a clear and compelling reason, the public reaction was swift, severe, and bipartisan. Even leaders of Nixon's own party signaled that they could not support him unless he appointed a credible replacement for Cox.

Where do such norms come from? The short answer is that they grow and develop organically over time. Generally, this occurs through a process of gradual accretion, but sometimes it occurs rapidly in response to highly salient historical episodes. In the late nineteenth and early twentieth centuries, the American people grew increasingly frustrated with corruption and lawlessness among their government officials. This frustration created a political opportunity for reformers who promised to do better and at least partially made good on this promise. Eventually, good government became a central tenet of the Progressive movement that swept American politics during this period.

Not all of the reforms pushed by this movement were good ones. Nor was the movement always successful in overcoming the powerful interests it opposed. The Teapot Dome scandal is a powerful testament to its limits. Even so, the Progressive movement made clear strides in reducing the rankest forms of government corruption. Those strides reset the expectations of the American people, who came to understand that real improvements were possible. Even high officials could be constrained by law and held accountable for breaking the law.[10]

Several decades later, the norms that emerged from this gradual process supplied a shared standard for judging Richard Nixon's lawlessness. In turn, the firm public reaction to Nixon's misconduct further strengthened the norms that would govern future generations. In particular, the outcry following the Saturday Night Massacre set a precedent that no president would dare to violate for more than two generations. Other smaller episodes have also set helpful precedents. For example, three past presidents have voluntarily testified under oath during special prosecutor investigations. This makes it considerably more difficult for future presidents to resist doing so.

In short, the past is still with us. It is a great and precious gift passed down to present-day Americans over many generations. Above all, that gift consists of a widely shared set of standards for acceptable behavior by public officials, including the president. Those standards are deeply rooted in long experience and made vivid by well-known historical episodes like the Saturday Night Massacre. They are the most potent weapon the American people possess for holding their presidents and other high government officials to account.

America, the Vulnerable

American norms of presidential behavior—and official conduct more generally—are among the strongest and most firmly established in the world. This is a large part of what legal scholars and others mean when they tout the strength of American democratic institutions. But the norms that undergird those institutions are also vulnerable to sudden collapse. That is because norms depend heavily on the assumption that they are widely shared. No senator wants to be the first to say it is acceptable for the president to fire a special prosecutor without good reason if every other senator—and most Americans—still believe that such conduct is beyond the pale of acceptable behavior.[11]

This reluctance can cause norms to persist even when most people no longer believe in them strongly. It also makes norms susceptible to what legal scholar Cass Sunstein has called a "norm cascade." If just a few prominent people break a norm and suffer no adverse consequence, the assumption that the norm is widely shared can crumble rapidly. This may lead others, who would previously have subscribed to the norm out of social conformity, to abandon it in droves. As Sunstein notes, "something of this kind happened with the attack on apartheid in South Africa, the fall of Communism, the election of Ronald Reagan, and the rise of the feminist movement." Many revolutions seem to result from a similar dynamic, which political scientists have dubbed a "regime change cascade."[12]

The implications for special prosecutors are straightforward and troubling. If a president defies or fires a special prosecutor and gets away with it, the norms against this behavior might be exposed as weak. That exposure might lead others to question these norms, resulting in a downward spiral or cascade in which the norms ultimately collapse completely. Such an outcome would permit the president who initiated the cascade to escape accountability. This would also make it far harder for the American people to hold future presidents accountable. The norms that made this possible in the past would no longer exist. They would have to be recreated from scratch.

This is another reason that the importance of restraining a lawless president should transcend partisanship. If a president of one party gets away with lawbreaking today, a president of the other party can more easily get away with it tomorrow. The risk of a self-reinforcing downward spiral is real and dangerous.

Such a cascade could, in theory, occur at any time. It takes only a few bold first movers who are willing test the strength of well-established norms. But two interconnected features of contemporary American politics make this an especially acute concern today. The first is the rise of political populism, embodied by but not limited to President Trump. The second is the intensely polarized character of contemporary partisan politics, which legal scholars and political scientists have dubbed "hyperpolarization."

An essential characteristic of populism of all forms is its willingness to upend the established order. Another is the outsized faith populist movements place in charismatic leaders. This makes populist leaders especially likely to test limits that previous presidents have taken for granted. Hyperpolarization substantially increases the risk that voters and public officials will respond in rigidly partisan fashion, excusing the violation of norms by presidents of their own party while denouncing it in presidents of the opposing party.[13]

There are already worrisome signs of this dynamic at work. From his arrival on the national political scene, Donald Trump smashed through one well-established norm after another. He mocked a disabled reporter, ridiculed a war hero senator, condoned violence against protestors, and took racial demagoguery to levels not seen since the Jim Crow era. During the 2016 presidential primary, Trump's fellow Republican candidates frequently criticized this behavior, as did other elites within the Republican Party.

This criticism continued more fitfully during the early months of his administration. But as Trump's presidency wore on, critical Republican voices grew fewer and farther between. By his second year in office, they were mostly confined to lame ducks like senators Bob Corker and Jeff Flake. In such an environment, it is difficult to imagine the supporters of a populist president punishing him for firing a special prosecutor—or otherwise abusing his power for personal or partisan ends. That should scare any American who cares about the rule of law.[14]

For good or ill, the resolution of these issues today will have long-lasting effects on American democratic norms. Those effects will be determined in part by the high visibility of special prosecutors and in part by the populism and hyperpolarization of contemporary American politics. But this is just a fancy way of saying that it is up to the American people. We will get exactly the presidency—and the democracy—we deserve. Let us choose wisely.

NOTES

Introduction

1. Southern Pacific Company v. Jensen, 244 U.S. 205, 222 (1917) (Holmes, J., dissenting); Oliver Wendell Holmes, Jr., "The Path of the Law," 10 *Harvard Law Review* 457 (1897).

Chapter 1

1. 28 C.F.R. § 600.4(a); Justice Department, *U.S. Attorney's Manual* 9-200.1.
2. Donald Smaltz, "The Independent Counsel: A View from Inside," 86 *Georgetown Law Journal* 2307 (1988).
3. Richard Ben-Veniste & George Frampton, Jr., *Stonewall* (1977).
4. Justice Department, *Prosecution of Public Corruption Cases* (1988).
5. Smaltz 1998; Lawrence Walsh, *Firewall: The Iran-Contra Conspiracy and Cover-up* (1997).
6. Ben-Veniste & Frampton 1977.
7. *Id.*
8. Smaltz 1998.
9. *Id.*
10. Marc Fisher, "Starr Warriors," *Washington Post*, February 3, 1998.
11. Frank Newport, "Starr's Tenure as Independent Counsel Marked by Strongly Unfavorable Public Opinion," Gallup News Service, October 19, 1999.
12. Benjamin Wittes, *Starr: A Reassessment* (2002).
13. Smaltz 1998.
14. Katy Harriger, *The Special Prosecutor in American Politics* (2d ed. 2000).
15. Cass Sunstein, *Impeachment: A Citizen's Guide* (2017).
16. Smaltz 1998.

Chapter 2

1. *The Papers of Ulysses S. Grant*, vol. 27, *January 1, 1876–October 31, 1876* (2005).
2. Ron Chernow, *Grant* (2017).

3. *Id.*; Timothy Rives, "Grant, Babcock, and the Whiskey Ring," 32 *Prologue*, 2000, https://www.archives.gov/publications/prologue/2000/fall/whiskey-ring-1.html; Lucius E. Guese, "St. Louis and the Great Whisky Ring," 36 *Missouri Historical Review* 160 (1942).

4. *The Papers of Ulysses S. Grant*, vol. 26, *1875* (2003).

5. *Id.*

6. *Id.*; Guese 1942; Rives 2000.

7. *Id.; St. Louis Globe-Democrat*, February 8, 1876.

8. Letter from William D. W. Barnard, Kirkwood, Missouri, to Ulysses S. Grant (July 19, 1875), in *The Papers of Ulysses S. Grant*, vol. 26 .

9. Chernow 2017; Rives 2000.

10. *The Papers of Ulysses S. Grant*, vol. 27; Rives 2000.

11. *Id.; New York Herald*, February 13, 1876.

12. *The Papers of Ulysses S. Grant*, vol. 27; Rives 2000; Chernow 2017.

13. *St. Louis Globe-Democrat*, February 18, 1876; Rives 2000; Guese 1942; Chernow 2017.

14. Rives 2000; Jennifer Hopper, "Reexamining the Nineteenth-Century Presidency and Partisan Press: The Case of President Grant and the Whiskey Ring Scandal," 42 *Social Science History* 109–133 (2018).

15. Laton McCartney, *The Teapot Dome Scandal: How Big Oil Bought the Harding White House and Tried to Steal the Country* (2014).

16. *Id.*; Gordon R. Owen, *The Two Alberts: Fountain and Flood* (1996).

17. McCartney 2014.

18. *Id.*; M. R. Werner & John Starr, *The Teapot Dome Scandal* (1959).

19. Bruce Bliven, "Tempest over Teapot," 16 *American Heritage* 1 (1965); McCartney 2014.

20. Burl Noggle, *Teapot Dome* (1962); McCartney 2014.

21. *Id.*; Congressional Record, April 28, 1922; "The Famous Five," https://www.senate.gov/artandhistory/history/common/briefing/Famous_Five_Seven.htm.

22. McCartney 2014; Werner & Starr 1959.

23. Werner & Starr 1959.

24. McCartney 2014; Werner & Starr 1959.

25. McCartney 2014.

26. *Id.*; Werner & Starr 1959; David A. Logan, "Historical Uses of a Special Prosecutor: The Administrations of Presidents Grant, Coolidge and Truman," Library of Congress, Congressional Research Service (1973).

27. McCartney 2014.

28. *Id.*

29. Alonzo Hamby, *Man of the People* (1995); David McCullough, *Truman* (1992).

30. *Id.*; Hamby 1995; *Time*, March 8, 1943.

31. Hamby 1995.

32. *Id.*; C. Vann Woodward, *Responses of the Presidents to Charges of Misconduct*, (1974); Logan 1973.

33. Hamby 1995; McCullough 1992; Logan 1973.
34. Hamby 1995.
35. *Id.*; McCullough 1992; Jules Abels, *The Truman Scandals* (1956).
36. Woodward 1974.

Chapter 3

1. Archibald Cox, Press Conference, National Press Club, CBS News Special Report, October 20, 1973; Ken Gormley, *Archibald Cox* (1997); Fred Emery, *Watergate: The Corruption of American Politics and the Fall of Richard Nixon* (1994) [the latter two sources currently appear for the first time in Ch.3, n. 3; those citations should be replaced with short form citations].
2. Gormley 1997; Emery 1994.
3. Bob Woodward & Carl Bernstein, *The Final Days: The Classic, Behind-the-Scenes Account of Richard Nixon's Last Days in the White House* (1976); Gormley 1997.
4. Cox Press Conference 1973.
5. Woodward & Bernstein 1976; Emery 1994.
6. Woodward & Bernstein 1976; Emery 1994.
7. Letter from James McCord to Judge John Sirica, March 19, 1973; Emery 1994.
8. McCord Letter 1973; Emery 1994.
9. Emery 1994.
10. Emery 1994; Richard Ben-Veniste & George Frampton, Jr., *Stonewall* (1977)
11. Emery 1994; Woodward & Bernstein 1976.
12. Emery 1994.
13. Richard Nixon, Presidential Address, April 30, 1973.
14. Woodward & Bernstein 1976; Emery 1994.
15. Gormley 1997.
16. *Id.*
17. Emery 1994.
18. Gormley 1997.
19. Ben-Veniste & Frampton 1977.
20. *Id.*
21. Gormley 1997; Emery 1994.
22. Ben-Veniste & Frampton 1977.
23. *Id.*; Gormley 1997.
24. Woodward & Bernstein 1976.
25. Emery 1994; "Sam Ervin (1896-1985)" in *The Watergate Files*, www.fordlibrarymuseum.gov.
26. Emery 1994.
27. *Id.*
28. *Id.*; Ben-Veniste & Frampton 1977.
29. Bob Woodward, *The Last of the President's Men* (2014); Emery 1994.
30. *Id.*; Woodward 2014.

31. Gormley 1997.
32. Stanley Kutler, *Watergate: A Brief History with Documents* (2d ed. 2009).
33. Gary Wills, "The Strange Case of Jefferson's Subpoena," *New York Review of Books*, May 2, 1974; Gormley 1997.
34. Gormley 1997; Emery 1994; Nixon v. Sirica, 487 F.2d 700 (1973).
35. Gormley 1997.
36. *Id.*; Emery 1994.
37. Gormley 1997; Ben-Veniste & Frampton 1977.
38. Gormley 1997.
39. *Id.*
40. Woodward & Bernstein 1976; Gormley 1997; Emery 1994.
41. Gormley 1997; Woodward & Bernstein 1976.
42. *Id.*; Ben-Veniste & Frampton 1977
43. Gormley 1997; Emery 1994; Leon Jaworski, *The Right and the Power: The Prosecution of Watergate* (1977).
44. Woodward & Bernstein 1976.
45. *Id.*; Emery 1994.

Chapter 4

1. Congressional Record, October 26, 1973, p. 35076; Katy Harriger, *The Special Prosecutor in American Politics* (2d ed. 2000).
2. *Id.*; Terry Eastland, *Ethics, Politics, and the Independent Counsel: Executive Power, Executive Vice 1793–1989* (1989).
3. Harriger 2000; U.S. Congress, Senate, Committee on Governmental Affairs, *Public Officials Integrity Act of 1977, Blind Trusts and Other Conflict of Interest Matters*, 95th Cong., 1st sess., 1977, statement of Lawton Chiles.
4. Ethics in Government Act of 1978, 28 U.S.C. §§ 591–9; Harriger 2000; Eastland 1989.
5. Harriger 2000; Smaltz 1998; Brett M. Kavanaugh, "The President and the Independent Counsel," 86 *Georgetown Law Journal* 2133 (1998).
6. Harriger 2000; Smaltz 1998; Kavanaugh 1998.
7. Harriger 2000; Kavanaugh 1998; Theodore Draper, *A Very Thin Line: The Iran-Contra Affair* (1991).
8. President William Jefferson Clinton, *Statement on Signing the Independent Counsel Reauthorization Act of 1994*, June 30, 1994.
9. Ken Gormley, *The Death of American Virtue: Clinton vs. Starr* (2010); Jeffrey Toobin, *A Vast Conspiracy: The Real Story of the Sex Scandal That Nearly Brought Down a President* (1999).
10. Gormley 2010; Toobin 1999.
11. Gormley 2010.
12. *Id.*

13. Gormley 2010; James McDougal & Curtis Wilkie, *Arkansas Mischief: The Birth of a National Scandal* (1998).
14. Gormley 2010; Jeff Gerth, "Clinton Joined S & L Operator in Ozark Real-Estate Venture," *New York Times*, March 8, 1992.
15. Gormley 2010; Toobin 1999.
16. Gormley 2010; James B. Stewart, *Blood Sport: The President and His Adversaries* (1997).
17. Gormley 2010; Toobin 1999.
18. Gormley 2010; Toobin 1999.
19. Gormley 2010; Toobin 1999.
20. Gormley 2010; Toobin 1999.
21. Gormley 2010; Toobin 1999.
22. Gormley 2010; Toobin 1999; Benjamin Wittes, *Starr: A Reassessment* (2002).
23. Gormley 2010; Toobin 1999.
24. Gormley 2010; Toobin 1999; *In re* Madison Guaranty Savings and Loan Ass'n, 1994 WL 913274 (D.C. Cir.).
25. Gormley 2010; Toobin 1999.
26. Gormley 2010; Wittes 2002; Toobin 1999.
27. Wittes 2002; Jacob Stein, Remarks at Sixty-Seventh Judicial Conference of the Fourth Circuit, June 27, 1997, published at 54 *Washington & Lee Law Review* 1515 (1997).
28. Cox 1997; Gormley 2010.
29. *Id.*
30. *Id.*
31. *Id.*
32. *Id.*
33. *Id.*; Toobin 1999.
34. Gormley 2010.
35. Id.; Wittes 2002; Toobin 1999.
36. Gormley 2010; Toobin 1999.
37. Gormley 2010; Wittes 2002; Toobin 1999.
38. Gormley 2010; Wittes 2002; Toobin 1999.
39. Gormley 2010; Wittes 2002; Lawrence E. Walsh, "Kenneth Starr and the Independent Counsel Act," *New York Review of Books*, March 5, 1998.
40. Gormley 2010; Wittes 2002.
41. Gormley 2010; Wittes 2002.
42. Newport 1999; "Presidential Approval Ratings—Bill Clinton," Gallup News Service, http://news.gallup.com/poll/116584/presidential-approval-ratings-bill-clinton.aspx.
43. *The Future of the Independent Counsel Act*, Hearings before the Senate Committee on Governmental Affairs, February 24, March 3, 17, 24, and April 14, 1999.

Chapter 5

1. Adam Rubenstein, "Neal Katyal: 'At Times, President Trump Has Behaved Far Worse Than Nixon Did,'" *Weekly Standard*, February 18, 2018.
2. Rubenstein 2018; *Washington Post*, "Whorunsgov: Neal Katyal"; Lenore Adkins, "Neal Katyal: From Debate Team to House of Cards," *Big Law Business*, November 4, 2016.
3. Rubenstein 2018; Neal Katyal, "Trump or Congress Can Still Block Robert Mueller. I Know. I Wrote the Rules," *Washington Post*, May 19, 2017; Adkins 2016; Akhil Reed Amar & Neal Kumar Katyal, "Executive Privileges and Immunities: The *Nixon* and *Clinton* Cases," 108 *Harvard Law Review* 701 (1995).
4. Rubenstein 2018; Katyal 2017.
5. Rubenstein 2018; Katyal 2017.
6. Rubenstein 2018; Katyal 2017; Neal K. Katyal & Kenneth W. Starr, "A Better Way to Protect Mueller," *New York Times*, February 19, 2018.
7. Rubenstein 2018; James Robinson, "After the Independent Counsel Act: Where Do We Go from Here?," 51 *Hastings Law Journal* 733 (2000).
8. 28 C.F.R. § 600.10.
9. Rubenstein 2018; Robinson 2000.
10. 28 C.F.R. § 600.3.
11. 28 C.F.R. § 600.7–9.
12. Rubenstein 2018; Katyal & Starr 2018; Katyal 2017; 28 C.F.R. § 600.9.
13. Adkins 2016; Robinson 2000.
14. Sari Horwitz, "More Than 1,100 Law Professors Oppose Jeff Sessions's Nomination as Attorney General," *Washington Post*, January 3, 2017; Alan Neuhauser, "Showtime for Sessions," *U.S. News & World Report*, January 9, 2017.
15. Matt Apuzzo, "Specter of Race Shadows Jeff Sessions, Potential Trump Nominee for Cabinet," *New York Times*, November 16, 2016; Editorial: "What Are You Hiding, Jeff Sessions?," *New York Times*, January 8, 2017; Attorney General Confirmation Hearing, C-SPAN, January 10, 2017.
16. *Id.*; Sessions Responses to Leahy Questions for the Record, submitted January 17, 2017, www.judiciary.senate.gov.
17. Adam Entous et al., "Sessions Discussed Trump Campaign–Related Matters with Russian Ambassador, U.S. Intelligence Intercepts Show," *Washington Post*, July 21, 2017; Julian Borger, "Jeff Sessions Shifts Ground on Russia Contacts under Senate Questioning," *Guardian*, October 18, 2017.
18. Tal Koppan, "Marco Rubio on World Leaders: Vladimir Putin a 'Gangster,' Kim Jong Un a 'Lunatic,'" *CNN Politics*, August 28, 2016; "Trump: 'Putin Called Me a Genius,'" Reuters Video, February 16, 2016.
19. Michael Crowley & Tyler Pager, "Trump Urges Russia to Hack Clinton's Email," *Politico*, July 27, 2016.

20. John Sweeney & Innes Bowen, "Joseph Mifsud: The Mystery Professor behind Trump Russia Inquiry," *BBC News*, March 21, 2018; Sharon LaFraniere et al., "How the Russia Inquiry Began: A Campaign Aide, Drinks and Talk of Political Dirt," *New York Times*, December 30, 2017.
21. *Id.*; Charlie Savage, "Assange, Avowed Foe of Clinton, Timed Email Release for Democratic Convention," *New York Times*, July 26, 2016.
22. Catherine Ho, "From Ukraine to Trump Tower, Paul Manafort Unafraid to Take on Controversial Jobs," *Washington Post*, April 7, 2016; David A. Graham, "How Did Any of These Guys Get Hired by Trump?," *Atlantic*, October 30, 2017.
23. Ho 2016; Franklin Foer, "The Plot against America," *Atlantic*, March 2018.
24. Ho 2016; Foer 2018.
25. Foer 2018.
26. *Id.*
27. *Id.*; Julia Ioffe & Franklin Foer, "Did Manafort Use Trump to Curry Favor with a Putin Ally?," *Atlantic*, October 2, 2017.
28. Rosalind S. Helderman & Karoun Demirjian, "Inside the June 2016 Trump Tower Meeting: A Droning Russian Lawyer and Hot Pink Jeans, but No Clinton Dirt," *Washington Post*, May 16, 2018.
29. *Id.*
30. *Id.*; Ryan Teague Beckwith, "Read Donald Trump's Subdued Victory Speech after Winning New Jersey," *Time*, June 8, 2016.
31. Helderman & Demirjian 2018.
32. *Id.*; Sharon LaFraniere & Andrew E. Kramer, "Talking Points Brought to Trump Tower Meeting Were Shared with Kremlin," *New York Times*, October 27, 2017; Irina Reznik & Henry Meyer, "Trump Jr. Hinted at Review of Anti-Russia Law, Moscow Lawyer Says," *Bloomberg Politics*, November 6, 2017.
33. Sharon LaFraniere et al., "Lobbyist at Trump Campaign Meeting Has a Web of Russian Connections," *New York Times*, August 21, 2017.
34. Reznik & Meyer 2017; Julia Glum, "Did Trump Know Donald Jr. Met with Russia? Timeline Shows He Promised a Clinton Bombshell the Same Week," *Newsweek*, July 13, 2017.
35. Ned Parker et al., "Trump Campaign Had at Least 18 Undisclosed Contacts with Russians: Sources," *Reuters World News*, May 17, 2017.
36. *Russian Targeting of Election Infrastructure during the 2016 Election: Summary of Initial Findings and Recommendations*, Senate Intelligence Committee, May 8, 2018.
37. Intelligence Community Assessment, *Assessing Russian Activities in Recent U.S. Elections*, January 6, 2017; Michael S. Schmidt et al., "Intercepted Russian Communications Part of Inquiry into Trump Associates," *New York Times*, January 19, 2017; Remarks by President Trump in Press Gaggle aboard Air Force One en route to Hanoi, Vietnam, November 11, 2017; "Donald Trump on Russia, Advice from Barack Obama and How He Will Lead," *Time*,

December 7, 2016; Mary Louise Kelly, "White House Admits National Security Adviser Spoke with Russia," NPR, February 10, 2017; Russell Berman, "It's Official: The FBI Is Investigating Trump's Links to Russia," *Atlantic*, March 20, 2017.

38. Adam Entous et al., "Sessions Met with Russian Envoy Twice Last Year, Encounters He Later Did Not Disclose," *Washington Post*, March 1, 2017; Mark Landler and Eric Lichtblau, "Jeff Sessions Recuses Himself from Russia Inquiry," *New York Times*, March 2, 2017.

39. Michael D. Shear & Matt Apuzzo, "F.B.I. Director James Comey Is Fired by Trump," *New York Times*, May 9, 2017; "President Trump: 'This Russia Thing Is a Made Up Story,'" *NBC Nightly News with Lester Holt*, May 11, 2017; Michael S. Schmidt, "Comey Memo Says Trump Asked Him to End Flynn Investigation," *New York Times*, May 16, 2016; Dylan Matthews, "Law Professor: 'If the Allegations Are True, Trump Has Committed a Serious Federal Crime,'" *Vox*, May 16, 2017.

40. Devlin Barrett et al., "Deputy Attorney General Appoints Special Counsel to Oversee Probe of Russian Interference in Election," *Washington Post*, May 18, 2017; Michael S. Schmidt & Julie Hirschfeld Davis, "Trump Asked Sessions to Retain Control of Russia Inquiry after His Recusal," *New York Times*, May 29, 2018; J. Weston Phippen, "Who Is Rod Rosenstein?," *Atlantic*, May 11, 2017.

41. Joseph Tafani et al., "Special Counsel Named to Head Russia Investigation; White House Caught by Surprise," *Los Angeles Times*, May 17, 2017.

42. Philip Bump, "Newt Gingrich on Special Investigators, Then and Now," *Washington Post*, June 12, 2017.

43. *Id.*

44. Eli Watkins, "Some of the Times Trump Has Called Russia Probe a 'Witch Hunt,'" CNN, January 11, 2018; Brian Mann, "'None of This Is Real': Conservative Media React to Mueller Indictments," NPR, October 31, 2017; Catherine Herridge & Alex Pappas, "Nunes: FBI May Have Violated Criminal Statutes in FISA Application to Spy on Trump Adviser Carter Page," *Fox News*, March 1, 2018; Samantha Schmidt, "Trump Touts Hannity's Show on 'Deep State Crime Families' Led by Mueller, Comey and Clintons," *Washington Post*, April 12, 2018.

45. Jennifer Agiesta, "CNN Poll: Republicans Shifting Negative on Mueller's Investigation," CNN, May 10, 2018; Toluse Olorunnippa & Steven T. Dennis, "Most Republicans Silent in Face of Trump's Attacks on Mueller," *Bloomberg Politics*, March 19, 2018.

Chapter 6

1. Reuters, "Donald Trump: 'I Could Shoot Somebody and I Wouldn't Lose Any Voters,'" January 24, 2016; Andrew Crespo, "The Road to *United States v. Trump* Is Paved with Prosecutorial Discretion," *Take Care*, May 21, 2017;

Susan Low Bloch, "Foreword: Can We Indict a Sitting President?," 2 *Nexus* 7 (1997).

2. Richard Ben-Veniste & George Frampton, Jr., *Stonewall* (1977); Bob Woodward & Carl Bernstein, *The Final Days: The Classic, Behind-the-Scenes Account of Richard Nixon's Last Days in the White House* (1976).

3. Ben-Veniste & Frampton 1977; John Herbers, "Nixon Names Saxbe Attorney General; Jaworski Appointed Special Prosecutor," *New York Times*, November 2, 1973.

4. Ben-Veniste & Frampton 1977.

5. John Hart Ely, *Memorandum to Special Prosecutor Archibald Cox on the Legality of Calling President Nixon before a Grand Jury* (1973); Ben-Veniste & Frampton 1977.

6. *Id.*; Woodward & Bernstein 1976; Leon Jaworski, *The Right and the Power* (1977).

7. Ben-Veniste & Frampton 1977.

8. *Id.*; Watergate Special Prosecution Force, Memorandum, "Recommendation for Action by the Watergate Grand Jury," February 12, 1974.

9. *Id.*.

10. *Id.*

11. *Id.*

12. Ben-Veniste & Frampton 1977.

13. *Id.*

14. *Id.*; Pinkerton v. United States, 328 U.S. 640 (1946); Federal Rules of Evidence 803.

15. Ben-Veniste & Frampton 1977.

16. *Id.*; Jaworski 1977.

17. Ben-Veniste & Frampton 1977.

18. *Id.*; Fred Emery, *Watergate: The Corruption of American Politics and the Fall of Richard Nixon* (1994); Woodward & Bernstein 1976.

19. Ben-Veniste & Frampton 1977.

20. *Id.*

21. *Id.*

22. *Id.*

23. *Id.*; "Some Lessons in Civics from Two American Juries," *People*, March 18, 1974.

24. Ken Gormley, *The Death of American Virtue: Clinton vs. Starr* (2010); Don Van Natta, Jr., "Starr Is Weighing Whether to Indict Sitting President," *New York Times*, January 31, 1999.

25. Gormley 2010; Van Natta 1999.

26. Gormley 2010; Van Natta 1999.

27. Gormley 2010; Ben-Veniste & Frampton 1977.

28. Van Natta 1999; Ronald D. Rotunda, Memorandum to Independent Counsel Kenneth Starr Re "Indictability of the President," May 13, 1998.

29. David Corn, "Starr's Right-Hand Man," *Nation*, February 4, 1999.

30. Rotunda 1998.
31. Morrison v. Olson, 487 U.S. 654 (1988); Office of Legal Counsel Memorandum, "A Sitting President's Amenability to Indictment and Criminal Prosecution," October 16, 2000.
32. *Id.*; Rotunda 1998.
33. Benjamin Wittes, *Starr: A Reassessment* (2002); Van Natta 1999.
34. *Id.*; Jaworski 1977; Ben-Veniste & Frampton 1977.
35. 28 C.F.R. § 600.7.
36. Ryan Goodman, "Robert Mueller Has the Authority to Name Donald Trump an Unindicted Co-conspirator," *Slate*, October 29, 2017; James B. Jacobs, "Can Trump Be Named as an 'Unindicted Coconspirator'?," September 5, 2017; U.S. Attorneys' Manual 9-11.130.
37. Ben-Veniste & Frampton 1977; Watergate Special Task Force Memorandum 1974; Ryan Goodman & Alex Whiting, "An Untold Option for Mueller: Grand Jury 'Presentment' as an Alternative to Indicting Trump," *Just Security*, August 16, 2017.

Chapter 7

1. Clifford S. Fishman & Anne T. McKenna, *7 Jones on Evidence* § 55:2 (2017); United States v. Nixon, 418 U.S. 683 (1974).
2. *Id.*; Mark J. Rozell, "Executive Privilege and the Modern Presidents: In Nixon's Shadow," 83 *Minnesota Law Review* 1069 (1999).
3. *Id.*; Mark J. Rozell, "Executive Privilege and the Modern Presidents: In Nixon's Shadow," 83 *Minnesota Law Review* 1069 (1999).
4. Rozell 1999; Richard Ben-Veniste & George Frampton, Jr., *Stonewall* (1977); Lawrence Walsh, *Firewall: The Iran-Contra Conspiracy and Cover-up* (1997).
5. Warren Weaver, Jr., "High Court Hears Three Hours of Debate in Nixon Cases and Reserves Its Decision," *New York Times*, July 9, 1974.
6. Bob Woodward & Carl Bernstein, *The Final Days: The Classic, Behind-the-Scenes Account of Richard Nixon's Last Days in the White House* (1976); Ben-Veniste & Frampton 1977.
7. Fred Emery, *Watergate: The Corruption of American Politics and the Fall of Richard Nixon* (1994); Weaver 1974; Bob Dylan, "It's Alright Ma (I'm Only Bleedin')," *Bringing It All Back Home*, Columbia Records, 1965.
8. Woodward & Bernstein 1976.
9. *Id.*
10. *Id.*; Ben-Veniste & Frampton 1977; Leon Jaworski, *The Right and the Power: The Prosecution of Watergate* (1977).
11. Woodward & Bernstein 1976; Ben-Veniste & Frampton 1977; Jaworski 1977.
12. Woodward & Bernstein 1976; Ben-Veniste & Frampton 1977; Emery 1994.
13. Woodward & Bernstein 1976.
14. *Id.*

15. Woodward & Bernstein 1976; Ben-Veniste & Frampton 1977; Jaworski 1977.
16. Emery 1994; Ben-Veniste & Frampton 1977; Woodward & Bernstein 1976.
17. Woodward & Bernstein 1976; Ben-Veniste & Frampton 1977; Jaworski 1977.
18. Ben-Veniste & Frampton 1977.
19. Woodward & Bernstein 1976; Emery 1994.
20. Richard M. Nixon, Presidential Address, April 29, 1974.
21. James M. Naughton, "Nixon Will Give Edited Tape Transcripts to House, the Public; Notes Ambiguities. Insists He Is Innocent," *New York Times*, April 30, 1974; Woodward & Bernstein 1976.
22. Woodward & Bernstein 1976; Ben-Veniste & Frampton 1977; Emery 1994.
23. Woodward & Bernstein 1976; Ben-Veniste & Frampton 1977;, "Presidential Approval Ratings—Gallup Historical Statistics and Trends," Gallup News .
24. Ben-Veniste & Frampton 1977; United States v. Mitchell, 377 F. Supp. 1326 (D.D.C. 1974).
25. Ben-Veniste & Frampton 1977; Jaworski 1977.
26. Woodward & Bernstein 1976; Ben-Veniste & Frampton 1977; Jaworski 1977.
27. Ben-Veniste & Frampton 1977.
28. Lucas A. Power, Jr., *The Supreme Court and the American Elite, 1789–2008* (2011); Bob Woodward & Scott Armstrong, *The Brethren: Inside the Supreme Court* (1979).
29. Weaver 1974; Woodward & Bernstein 1976; Ben-Veniste & Frampton 1977.
30. Transcript of Oral Argument, United States v. Nixon 1974 (No. 73-1766).
31. *Id.*
32. *Id.*
33. *Id.*
34. *Id.*
35. *Id.*
36. *Id.*
37. *Id.*; Woodward & Bernstein 1976.
38. Transcript of Oral Argument, United States v. Nixon 1974 (No. 73-1766).
39. *Id.*
40. *Id.*
41. *Id.*
42. *Id.*
43. *Id.*; Ben-Veniste & Frampton 1977; Woodward & Bernstein 1976.
44. Transcript of Oral Argument, United States v. Nixon 1974 (No. 73-1766).
45. *Id.*
46. *Id.*
47. United States v. Nixon 1974; Woodward & Bernstein 1976; John A. Farrell, *Richard Nixon: The Life* (2017).
48. Ben-Veniste 1977; Woodward & Bernstein 1976; Emery 1994.
49. Emery 1994; Woodward & Bernstein 1976; Farrell 2017.

50. Rozell 1999; Heidi Kitrosser, "Secrecy and Separated Powers: Executive Privilege Revisited," 92 *Iowa Law Review* 489 (2007); Keith E. Whittington, "Don't Subpoena Testimony from the President," *Lawfare*, May 4, 2018.

51. Rozell 1999; Kitrosser 2007; Whittington 2018.

52. Whittington 2018; Joseph Story, *A Familiar Exposition of the Constitution of the United States: Containing a Brief Commentary with an Appendix* (1840); letter from Thomas Jefferson to George Hay, June 20, 1807.

53. Clinton v. Jones, 520 U.S. 681 (1997); United States v. Nixon 1974; Whittington 2018.

54. Rozell 1999; Ben-Veniste & Frampton 1977; Walsh 1997.

55. Rozell 1999; Whittington 2018.

56. Office of Legal Counsel Memorandum, "A Sitting President's Amenability to Indictment and Criminal Prosecution," October 16, 2000 (quoting unpublished Office of Legal Counsel Memorandum, "Constitutional Concerns Implicated by Demand for Presidential Evidence in a Criminal Prosecution," October 17, 1988); Douglas W. Kmiec & Ryan Goodman, "The Missing Justice Department Memo on Whether a President Can Be Subpoenaed to Testify in a Criminal Case," *Just Security*, May 17, 2018.

Chapter 8

1. Fred Emery, *Watergate: The Corruption of American Politics and the Fall of Richard Nixon* (1994); John A. Farrell, *Richard Nixon: The Life* (2017; House Judiciary Committee, Articles of Impeachment against President of the United States Richard M. Nixon, July 27, 1974.

2. Lawrence Walsh, *Firewall: The Iran-Contra Conspiracy and Cover-up* (1997); Lawrence Walsh, *Final Report of the Independent Counsel for Iran/Contra Matters*, August 4, 1993; "The Iran-Contra Affair 20 Years On: Documents Spotlight Roll of Reagan, Key Aides," National Security Archive Electronic Briefing Book No. 201, November 24, 2006.

3. Ken Gormley, *The Death of American Virtue: Clinton vs. Starr* (2010); House Judiciary Committee, Articles of Impeachment against President William Jefferson Clinton, December 12, 1998.

4. Michael S. Schmidt & Julie Hirschfeld David, "Trump Asked Sessions to Retain Control of Russia Inquiry after His Recusal," *New York Times*, May 29, 2018; Devlin Barrett et al., "Mueller Investigation Examining Trump's Apparent Efforts to Oust Sessions in July," *Washington Post*, February 28, 2018.

5. David B. Rivkin, Jr., & Lee A. Casey, "Can the President Obstruct Justice?," *Wall Street Journal*, December 10, 2017; Josh Blackman, "Obstruction of Justice and the Presidency: Part I," *Lawfare*, December 5, 2017; Saikrishna Prakash & John Yoo, "Can the President Obstruct Justice?," *National Review*, December 15, 2017; U.S. Constitution, Article II; Michael S. Schmidt et al., "Trump's

Lawyers, in Confidential Memo, Argue to Head Off a Historic Subpoena," *New York Times*, June 2, 2018.

6. Rivkin & Casey 2017; Blackman 2017; Prakash & Yoo 2017; *Frost/Nixon Interviews*, May 17, 1977.

7. Daniel Hemel & Eric Posner, "Presidential Obstruction of Justice," 106 *California Law Review* (forthcoming 2018); Barry H. Berke et al., "Presidential Obstruction of Justice: The Case of Donald Trump," Brookings Institute White Paper, October 10, 2017; Daniel Hemel, "Of Course the President Can Obstruct Justice," *Slate*, December 4, 2017.

8. Hemel & Posner 2018; 18 U.S.C. § 1503(a).

9. Hemel & Posner 2018; Walsh 1997; Walsh 1993.

10. Hemel & Posner 2018; United States v. Aguilar, 515 U.S. 593 (1995).

11. Stuart P. Green, "Uncovering the Cover-up Crimes," 42 *American Criminal Law Review* 9 (2005).

12. Daniel C. Richman & William J. Stuntz, "Al Capone's Revenge: An Essay on the Political Economy of Pretextual Prosecution, 105 *Columbia Law Review* 583 (2005); Harry Litman, "Pretextual Prosecution," 92 *Georgetown Law Journal* 1135 (2004).

13. Hemel & Posner 2018.

14. *Id.*; McCartney 2014.

15. Hemel & Posner 2018; McCartney 2014.

16. Hemel & Posner 2018; Richard Primus, "Motive Matters in Assessing the Travel Ban Case," *Take Care*, March 20, 2017.

17. Hemel & Posner 2018; Jess Bidgood, "Pennsylvania's Attorney General Is Convicted on All Counts," *New York Times*, August 15, 2017.

18. Hemel & Posner 2018; "Guidance Regarding Marijuana Enforcement," Justice Department Memorandum for All U.S. Attorneys, August 29, 2013.

19. Philip Shenon, "U.S. Tells Court Subpoena Errs In Deaver Case," *New York Times*, June 20, 1987; Eric Posner, "Why Obama Won't Prosecute Torturers," *Slate*, December 9, 2014; Hemel & Posner 2018.

20. *Id.*; Berke et al. 2017.

21. Hemel & Posner 2018.

22. *Id.*

23. *Id.*; 18 U.S.C. § 1503(a); United States v. Simmons, 591 F.2d 206 (3d Cir. 1979); 18 U.S.C. § 1512(c).

24. Farrell 2017; Richard Severo, "H. R. Haldeman, Nixon Aide Who Had Central Role in Watergate, Is Dead at 67," *New York Times*, November 13, 1993; Robyn Price Pierre, "How a Conservative Wins the Presidency in a Liberal Decade," *Atlantic*, July 9, 2016.

25. Transcript of a Recording of a Meeting between the President and H. R. Haldeman in the Oval Office on June 23, 1972, from 10:04 to 11:39 a.m.

26. *Id.*

27. *Id.*

28. *Id.*
29. *Id.*
30. *Id.*
31. *Id.*; Emery 1994; Woodward & Bernstein 1976; Richard Reeves, *President Nixon: Alone in the White House* (2001).
32. Emery 1994; Woodward & Bernstein 1976.
33. Nancy Gibbs, "The Currie Riddle," CNN, April 27, 1998; David Plotz, *Slate*, "Betty Currie, the Plight of the Presidential Secretary," February 8, 1998; "Betty Currie Oral History, Personal Secretary to the President," Presidential Oral Histories, Miller Center, University of Virginia, Charlottesville, Virginia.
34. "Excerpts from Betty Currie Testimony," *Washington Post*, October 2, 1998; Gormley 2011; Jeffrey Toobin, *A Vast Conspiracy: The Real Story of the Sex Scandal That Nearly Brought Down a President* (1999).
35. "Excerpts from Betty Currie Testimony" 1998.
36. *Id.*; Gormley 2011; Toobin 1999.
37. "Excerpts from Betty Currie Testimony 1998; Betty Currie Oral History 2006; Toobin 1999.
38. Gormley 2011; Toobin 1999.
39. James Comey, *A Higher Loyalty* (2018); "Resolute Desk," *White House Museum*, http://whitehousemuseum.org.
40. Comey 2018.
41. *Id.*; James Comey Memorandum, February 14, 2017.
42. Comey 2018; Colleen Shalby, "Timeline: What We Know about the Events Leading to Michael Flynn's Resignation," *Los Angeles Times*, February 14, 2017.
43. *Id.*; Comey 2018
44. *Id.*; 18 U.S.C. § 953; Daniel Hemel & Eric Posner, "Why the Trump Team Should Fear the Logan Act," *New York Times*, December 4, 2017.
45. Comey 2018.
46. *Id.*
47. *Id.*; Testimony of Former FBI Director James Comey, Senate Intelligence Committee, June 8, 2017.
48. Comey 2018; Gregory Krieg, "Tick-Tock: How Comey's Firing Played Out in Real Time," *CNN*, May 9, 2017; letter from President Donald J. Trump to James Comey, May 9, 2017.
49. Scott Detrow, "'Nothing Less Than Nixonian': Democrats React To Comey Firing," NPR, May 9, 2017; Evan Osnos, "How Comey's Firing Accelerates the Russia Investigation," *New Yorker*, May 10, 2017.
50. Matt Apuzzo et al., "Trump Told Russians That Firing 'Nut Job' Comey Eased Pressure from Investigation," *New York Times*, May 19, 2017.
51. Michael S. Schmidt, "Comey Memo Says Trump Asked Him to End Flynn Investigation," *New York Times*, May 16, 2017; Devlin Barrett et al., "Deputy Attorney General Appoints Special Counsel to Oversee Probe of Russian Interference in Election," *Washington Post*, May 18, 2017; U.S.

Justice Department, Appointment of Special Counsel to Investigate Russian Interference with the 2016 Presidential Election and Related Matters, Order No. 3915-2017, May 17, 2017.

52. Michael S. Schmidt, "Obstruction Inquiry Shows Trump's Struggle to Keep Grip on Russia Investigation," *New York Times*, January 4, 2018; Michael S. Schmidt and Julie Hirschfeld Davis, "Trump Asked Sessions to Retain Control of Russia Inquiry after His Recusal," *New York Times*, May 29, 2018; Jonathan Swan, "Trump Repeatedly Pressured Sessions on Mueller Investigation," *Axios*, May 31, 2018; Jonathan Mahler & Matt Flegenheimer, "What Donald Trump Learned from Joseph McCarthy's Right-hand Man," *New York Times*, June 20, 2016.

53. Hemel & Posner 2018; Kevin Johnson, "Special Counsel Robert Mueller Using Multiple Grand Juries in Russia Inquiry," *USA Today*, August 4, 2017.

54. Jonathan Turley, "Donald Trump's Clever Plan to Foil an Obstruction of Justice Charge," *USA Today*, May 31, 2018.

55. Lauren Peale, "Yes, a President Can Obstruct Justice, Legal Experts Say," *ABC News*, December 5, 2017; Aaron Blake, "Trump's Lawyer Says a President Can't Technically Obstruct Justice. Experts Say That's Fanciful," *Washington Post*, December 4, 2017; Scott Bomboy, "Can a President Obstruct Justice? The Legal Experts Have a Few Thoughts," *Constitution Daily*, December 4, 2017; Hemel & Posner 2018.

Chapter 9

1. 28 C.F.R. § 600 ; The Special Counsel Independence and Integrity Act (S.2644), 115th Congress.

2. Saikrishna Prakash & John Yoo, "Of Course Trump Can Fire Mueller. He Shouldn't," *New York Times*, April 13, 2018; Adrian Vermeule, "*Morrison v. Olson* Is Bad Law," *Lawfare*, June 9, 2017; Steven G. Calabresi and Kevin H. Rhodes, "The Structural Constitution: Unitary Executive, Plural Judiciary," 105 *Harvard Law Review* 1153 (1992).

3. U.S. Constitution, Article I, § 8, Clause 18; Earl C. Dudley, Jr., "*Morrison v. Olson*: A Modest Assessment," 38 *American University Law Review* 255 (1989); Jonathan L. Entin, "Separation of Powers, the Political Branches, and the Limits of Judicial Review," 51 *Ohio State Law Journal* 175 (1990); Victoria F. Nourse, "The Special Counsel: Can Congress Constitutionally Limit the President's Removal Power? The Radical Implications of Justice Scalia's Dissent in *Morrison v. Olson*," American Constitution Society White Paper (2018).

4. Dudley 1989; Entin 1990; Nourse 2018; Youngstown Sheet & Tube Co. v. Sawyer, 343 U.S. 579 (1952) (Jackson, J., concurring).

5. Morrison v. Olson, 487 U.S. 654 (1988).

6. Charles Fried, *Order and Law: Arguing the Reagan Revolution* (1991).

7. Stuart Taylor, Jr., "Justices Are Urged to Nullify Independent Prosecutor Law," *New York Times*, April 27, 1988.

8. Lois Romano, "Supreme Satisfaction," *Washington Post*, July 1, 1988.

9. *Id.*

10. Ryan C. Black & Ryan J. Owens, *The Solicitor General and the United States Supreme Court: Executive Influence and Judicial Decisions* (2012).

11. Stephen Skowronek, *Presidential Leadership in Political Time: Reprise and Reappraisal* (2008); Laura Kalman, *Right Star Rising: A New Politics, 1974–1980* (2010).

12. Patricia Sullivan, "Anne Gorsuch Burford, 62, Dies; Reagan EPA Director," *Washington Post*, July 22, 2004; Anne M. Burford & John Greenya, *Are You Tough Enough?: An Insider's View of Washington Power Politics* (1986).

13. Joanna Brenner, "Neil Gorsuch's Late Mother Almost Annihilated the EPA. Is History Repeating Itself?," *Newsweek*, February 1, 2017; Brady Dennis & Chris Mooney, "Neil Gorsuch's Mother Once Ran the EPA. It Didn't Go Well," *Washington Post*, February 1, 2017.

14. Brenner 2017; John Jones & Jack Smith, "Critics of EPA Are Right," *New York Times*, September 1, 1982.

15. "Justice Department Probe of EPA Clears Burford, 5 Others," United Press International, August 11, 1983; Eleanor Randolph, "Gorsuch Denies That Politics Sways EPA's Decisions," *Los Angeles Times*, February 10, 1983.

16. UPI 1983; Report on Investigation of the Role of the Justice Department in the Withholding of Environmental Protection Agency Documents from Congress, H.R. Rep. No. 99-435 (1985).

17. James Worsham, "EPA to Turn Over Files: Accord Could End Standoff with Congress," *Chicago Tribune*, February 19, 1983; Robert L. Jackson, "House Votes to Hold EPA Chief in Contempt over Files," *Los Angeles Times*, December 3, 1982; Burford & Greenya 1986.

18. Ronald J. Ostrow & Robert L. Jackson, "'Superfund' Probe Expanding," *Los Angeles Times*, March 11, 1983; Ronald J. Ostrow, "Independent Counsel Explains Why She Didn't Prosecute Figure in '83 EPA Probe," *Los Angeles Times*, March 21, 1989.

19. Office of Legal Counsel of the Justice Department, Oversight Hearings Before the Subcommittee on Monopolies and Commercial Law of the Committee on the Judiciary, House of Representatives, 98th Congress, March 10, 1983.

20. Ostrow 1989; H.R. Rep. No. 99-435.

21. *Id.*; Morrison v. Olson 1988.

22. Katy Harriger, *The Special Prosecutor in American Politics* (2d ed. 2000); Fried 1991.

23. Morrison v. Olson, Oral Argument Transcript; Linda Greenhouse, "The Chief Justice Has New Clothes," *New York Times*, January 22, 1995; "Supreme Court Chief Justice Rehnquist Dies," Associated Press, September 3, 2005.

24. Tammy A. Sarver et al., "The Attorney Gender Gap in U.S. Supreme Court Litigation," 91 *Judicature* 238 (2008); Adam Feldman, "A Dearth of Female Attorneys at Supreme Court Oral Arguments," *Empirical SCOTUS*, October 22, 1917; Romano 1988.
25. Morrison v. Olson, Oral Argument Transcript.
26. *Id.*; McCulloch v. Maryland, 17 U.S. 316 (1819).
27. Morrison v. Olson, Oral Argument Transcript.
28. *Id.*
29. *Id.*
30. *Id.*
31. Lochner v. New York, 198 U.S. 45 (1905) (Holmes, J., dissenting); Morrison v. Olson, Oral Argument Transcript.
32. *Id.*
33. *Id.*
34. *Id.*; Fried 1991.
35. Morrison v. Olson (Scalia, J., dissenting).
36. *Id.*
37. *Id.*
38. *Id.*; "In Conversation with Antonin Scalia," *New York Magazine*, October 6, 2013.
39. Vermeule 2017; Linda Greenhouse, "The Price of Good Intentions," *New York Times*, February 1, 1998.
40. Neal K. Katyal & Kenneth W. Starr, "A Better Way to Protect Mueller," *New York Times*, February 19, 2018; Vermeule 2017.

Epilogue

1. Plato, *The Republic* (trans. Allan Bloom, 3d ed. 2016).
2. Frank Newport, "History Shows That Presidential Job Approval Ratings Can Plummet Rapidly," Gallup News, February 11, 1998; David Coleman, "Nixon's Presidential Approval Ratings," *History in Pieces*, https://historyinpieces.com/research/nixon-approval-ratings.
3. Fred Emery, *Watergate: The Corruption of American Politics and the Fall of Richard Nixon* (1994).
4. *Id.*; John A. Farrell, *Richard Nixon: The Life* (2017); Woodward & Bernstein 1976.
5. Jennifer Hopper, "Reexamining the Nineteenth-Century Presidency and Partisan Press: The Case of President Grant and the Whiskey Ring Scandal," 42 *Social Science History* 109–133 (2018); Ron Chernow, *Grant* (2017).
6. Hopper 2018; Chernow 2017.
7. Chernow 2017; Timothy Rives, "Grant, Babcock, and the Whiskey Ring," 32 *Prologue*, 2000, https://www.archives.gov/publications/prologue/2000/fall/whiskey-ring-1.html.

8. Chernow 2017; Rives 2000; Michael F. Holt, *By One Vote: The Disputed Presidential Election of 1876* (2008); Eric Foner, *Reconstruction: America's Unfinished Revolution, 1863–1877* (1988).

9. Akhil Amar, *America's Unwritten Constitution: The Precedents and Principles We Live By* (2011); Adrian Vermeule, "Conventions of Agency Independence," 113 *Columbia Law Review* 1163 (2013); Keith E. Whittington, "The Status of Unwritten Constitutional Conventions in the United States," 2013 *University of Illinois Law Review* 1847; Richard H. McAdams, "The Origin, Development, and Regulation of Norms," 96 *Michigan Law Review* 338, 340 (1997).

10. Maureen A. Flanagan, *America Reformed: Progressives and Progressivisms, 1890s–1920s* (2007); Doris Kearns Goodwin, *The Bully Pulpit: Theodore Roosevelt, William Howard Taft, and the Golden Age of Journalism* (2013); Richard Hofstader, *The Age of Reform: From Bryan to FDR* (1955).

11. Cass R. Sunstein, "Social Norms and Social Roles," 96 *Columbia Law Review* 903 (1996); McAdams 1997.

12. Sunstein 1996; Henry E. Hale, "Regime Change Cascades: What We Have Learned from the 1848 Revolutions to the 2011 Arab Uprisings," 16 *Annual Review of Political Science* 331 (2013).

13. Jan-Werner Müller, *What Is Populism?* (2016); Margaret Canovan, *Populism* (1981); Gino Germani, *Authoritarianism, Fascism, and National Populism* (1978); Aziz Z. Huq, "The People against the Constitution," 116 *Michigan Law Review* 1123 (2018); Richard H. Pildes, "Why the Center Does Not Hold: The Causes of Hyperpolarized Democracy in America," 99 *California Law Review* 273 (2011).

14. Emily Bazelon, "How Do We Contend with Trump's Defiance of 'Norms'?," *New York Times Magazine*, July 11, 2017; Jack Goldsmith, "Will Donald Trump Destroy the Presidency?," *Atlantic*, October 2017; Steven Levitsky & Daniel Ziblatt, *How Democracies Die* (2018).

INDEX